The Little Red Book

of

Wisdom

THE LITTLE RED BOOK

of

WISDOM

MARK DeMOSS

Published by
THOMAS NELSON™
Since 1798

www.thomasnelson.com

Published in Nashville, Tennessee, by Thomas Nelson, Inc.

Published in association with the literary agency of Wolgemuth & Associates, Inc.

Thomas Nelson, Inc. titles may be purchased in bulk for educational, business, fundraising, or sales promotional use. For information, please email SpecialMarkets@ThomasNelson.com.

Scripture quotations taken from *The Message* by Eugene H. Peterson, Copyright © 1993, 1994, 1995, 1996, 2000. Used by permission of NavPress Publishing Group. All rights reserved.

Scripture quotations taken from the *HOLY BIBLE: NEW INTERNATIONAL VERSION*®. Copyright © 1973, 1978, 1984 by International Bible Society. Used by permission of Zondervan Publishing House. All rights reserved.

Scripture quotations taken from *THE NEW KING JAMES VERSION*. Copyright © 1982 by Thomas Nelson, Inc. Used by permission. All rights reserved.

Scripture quotations taken from the *NEW AMERICAN STANDARD BIBLE*®, Copyright © The Lockman Foundation 1960, 1962, 1963, 1968, 1971, 1972, 1973, 1975, 1977. Used by permission.

Cover design: Identity Studios, Inc.

Library of Congress Cataloging-in-Publication Data

DeMoss, Mark.
    The little red book of wisdom / Mark DeMoss.
        p. cm.
    ISBN-13: 978-0-7852-2168-5 (hardcover)
    ISBN-10: 0-7852-2168-9
    1. Conduct of life. 2. Success—Religious aspects—Christianity. 3. Success in business. 4. Success. I. Title.
    BJ1521.D46 2006
    170'.44—dc22

                                    2006032324

Printed in the United States of America

07 08 09 10 RRD 5 4 3 2 1

Dedication

He who finds a wife finds a good thing, and
obtains favor from the Lord.
The Bible, The Book of Proverbs

Children are a gift of the Lord.
The Bible, The Book of Psalms

I dedicate this book to the four most important people in the world: to April, my wife of nineteen years, and to our three teenagers, Georgia, Mookie, and Madison. If wisdom is a journey, and I believe it is, I would rather travel it with these four than with anyone else.

The world's library shelves already bulge with books on marriage, and this is not another one. This is a dedication of a book on wisdom to the woman who has taught me volumes about life. From April I have learned the beauty of serving with no motive but to serve. From her I've learned that we can accomplish more together than either of us could do alone in twice the time. From April, I've learned to live what really matters.

April lives her priorities, and her priorities are us—our

children and me. That devotion returns to her in full measure. For my years with April, *because* of April, I am a wiser and better man. Thank you, my Love You changed my life forever, and each new day I love you more than the day before.

———

From the first, my passion to write this book has had dual engines: to thank my father and to prepare my boy and two girls in the way my father prepared me. The world changes with every generation, but thankfully, life's surest principles do not.

Georgia, you are wise beyond your years, and I marvel at your maturity, your gentle spirit, and your love for others. You are an example to me in many ways, and I love you, girl.

Mookie, even as a young teen, you exhibit great wisdom. Your daily practice of reading in the Book of Proverbs amazes me. I'm proud of you and love every minute we spend together.

Madison, you stole my heart as a baby and a little smile still appears just to think of you. Few people greet every day as you do, as an adventure and gift, and that's what you are to me. I love you, Maddie.

If I could teach all of you but one thing about wisdom, it would be to follow the Source. My love follows you always; keep loving each other, and thank you for loving and blessing me as you have and do. I'm proud of each of you.

Acknowledgments

Writing a book doesn't happen without help. This is undoubtedly truer for a person writing their first book, so I'd like to thank several people.

Thank you, Thomas Nelson Publishers, for believing in me, and this subject, enough to put your name and resources behind this book. I am grateful.

Thank you, Robert Wolgemuth, for showing me how to advance an idea and a vision to a book that is actually publishable. Thank you, Nancy Lovell, for your writing help; your touch improved every page.

I am backed by an incredible team at The DeMoss Group, a team that had less of me during the writing of this book. Thank you, Christy Lynn, Frank, Gillian, Jeff, Jennifer, Jeremy, Jessica, Karen, Kristen, Lily, Michelle, Regina, Sherry, Sintya, Tiffanie, Todd, and Tracy. And a special thanks to my wonderful assistant, Brenda, and my colleague Beth, who has worked with me for a dozen years.

Over the years, I have also benefitted from incredible opportunities and experiences from our clients. Thank you for your confidence and trust in me and my team—I take neither for granted. Thank you, Franklin Graham, for believing in me when The DeMoss Group was just me and an assistant.

Thank you, Jerry Falwell, for investing in me as a young college graduate and giving me a lifetime of experiences in just eight years—you're a better friend than I deserve. And thank you, Mrs. Falwell, for treating me like one of your sons. James Merritt and Andy Stanley are two pastors full of wisdom. During the past sixteen years I have learned much from the teaching of these great men. Thank you.

I've been blessed with the greatest in-laws anyone could ever ask or pray for. Thank you, Art and Angela, for your love and your enthusiasm for this book.

On a number of pages of this book, I write about my late father. Though he died in 1979, he remains the wisest person in my life. We shared only seventeen years on this earth, but I owe him much. Indeed, he is an impetus for this book. Thank you, Dad, for modeling a heart and a life of wisdom.

My mother is a remarkable woman who woke up one September morning in 1979 as a forty-year-old widow with seven children, one of whom would die seven years later. Not until I was married and had children of my own could I appreciate the difference between losing a spouse and a son, and losing a parent and a sibling. Thank you, Mother, for loving me through every stage.

Thank you, April . . . for everything.

Above all, thank you, Lord, for picking me up and placing me where you have—like a turtle on a fencepost.

*Wisdom is the principal thing;
therefore get wisdom.*

The Bible, The Book of Proverbs

Contents

CONTENTS

PART TWO: WISDOM FOR YOUR PERSONAL LIFE

CONTENTS

Do you see a man wise in his own eyes?
There is more hope for a fool than for him.
The Bible, The Book of Proverbs

What in the world qualifies me to write a book about wisdom? From the beginning, let me state clearly that wisdom is a journey and not a destination. On my journey—ahead of some, behind others—I have no illusions about having arrived. Wisdom is generally associated with gray hair, and though some gray is sprinkling in, I am still a relatively young man with much to learn.

The Hebrew word for wisdom means "skill in living," which suggests that time—years—is required to achieve it. Even then, it takes more than time. As evangelist and elder statesman Billy Graham once said, "Knowledge is horizontal, but wisdom is vertical—it comes down from above." In other words, God is the source of all wisdom.

There is one reason I wrote this book, my first ever, and

several reasons why I'm comfortable doing so. If only one copy existed, it would be for my three children: Georgia, Mookie (his nickname since he was an infant), and Madison. If these words help them on their paths through life, it will be worth every hour of writing.

Still, who am I to write on such a lofty subject? A few thoughts come to mind. First, a friend once told me that "wisdom is caught, not taught." If that's true, I've had the good fortune to catch some wisdom through exposure to and association with people much wiser than me.

Second, a career in public relations has heightened my regard for wisdom. To observe the power of public opinion, to have responsibility to respond to delicate media inquiries, to manage crises of every conceivable type, to participate in boardroom deliberations involving millions of dollars, thousands of employees, and the future of large organizations has taught me much about wisdom—and sometimes the lack of it.

In 1991, I founded a public relations firm called The DeMoss Group, and have been privileged to work closely with many of the world's most prominent religious organizations—advising and helping them manage and fulfill their goals and objectives. The DeMoss Group has grown into a team of talented men and women, all of whom teach me, and I am in their debt.

It seems every week I receive a phone call that goes something like this: "Mark, I'm on the board of an organization in the midst of a major transition of leadership, and I'd like to get your wisdom on it." Or, "Our event is going to be disrupted by protesters, and we want your counsel on how to handle it." Or, "We'd like to get your wisdom on a new initiative we're planning to launch that may be controversial."

Now, I certainly have no lock on wisdom, but I'm a good listener (I've devoted a full chapter to listening) and a person can learn a lot by listening. This book is an attempt to share some of what I've learned.

Third, I'm a student of the greatest wisdom textbook of all time, the Old Testament Book of Proverbs—written by King Solomon, who is still widely regarded as the wisest man who ever lived. (Another full chapter is devoted to the reading and studying of Proverbs.) For half of my life, I have read a chapter of Proverbs a day, every single day—meaning I have been through the entire thirty-one-chapter book more than 250 times.

Finally, and most important, the Bible contains a most wonderful promise from God: "If any of you lacks wisdom, let him ask of God, who gives to all liberally and without reproach, and it will be given to him."

Solomon was the son of King David. One night God appeared to Solomon in a dream and told him that he could ask for and receive anything he wanted. That's quite an offer—and Solomon's answer is one of the Bible's great stories. Basically handed a blank check, Solomon asked God for *wisdom*—for a discerning heart to know how to govern the people in his charge.

God's reply tops even Solomon's request. God said He would give Solomon what he asked for; but because he requested wisdom and not a long life or wealth, he would also receive what he did *not* ask for. And God showered Solomon with riches and honor unequaled among kings in his lifetime.

My prayer, my request of God for years, has been for wisdom—to handle relationships well, to manage a business and advise clients, to be a good husband and father. Most days I begin by asking God for wisdom; most meetings I enter silently asking God for His insight. God honors His promise to provide wisdom to all who ask, and amazingly, the offer never expires.

And so I offer my observations on wisdom in the pages that follow. I am not the source of wisdom and never will be; but I eagerly study wise people, and I've organized my thoughts, experiences, and observations into this small collection. Everything foundational in my personal and professional life is recorded in this book. Beyond my three children, I would be encouraged if any reader gleans an insight or two and applies it to more skillful living. Wisdom guides and guards us. It calls out to all who listen, offering its services. It speaks to men and women, boys and girls. Its advice is universal, timeless, and foolproof.

Meanwhile, the gaining of wisdom is amazingly simple. A reader of any age can apply almost any of these principles in a matter of minutes: read a Proverb every day, listen more than you speak, write more letters, tell the truth always. Wisdom does not favor intelligence or education, affluence or sophistication; it calls to everyone, everywhere. We need only respond.

——— PART I ———

WISDOM FOR YOUR
PROFESSIONAL LIFE

Chapter 1

A MATTER OF DEATH AND LIFE

*No one can confidently say that he
will still be living tomorrow.*
Euripides

During the summer before my senior year in high school, I spent only a few days at home because my father had encouraged me to take a job with the Southwestern Company selling books door-to-door. My dad was my hero, and I agreed to the work unaware that it would mean thirteen-hour days for eight straight weeks with no breaks to see my family.

I hated being away from home. I hated that the time with Southwestern didn't allow me to join my parents and six brothers and sisters on vacation in the Caribbean. My father and I spoke each weekend by phone—he took great interest in my progress—but nothing could substitute for being with him.

I was back home that Friday in late August, just before

1

classes started for my senior year, when he and I met for lunch at the headquarters of National Liberty Corporation, the life insurance company he had founded and led to considerable success. I was always so proud to be his son when I walked through the beautiful corporate headquarters by his side. That day we talked about my plans for college and possibly for business later on.

The next day, Saturday, September 1, 1979, an ambulance sped to our home where my father had been playing tennis with three other men. One of them had rushed up to the house to make the emergency call. I didn't think to worry. Lots of men fall out of breath during exercise. Dad was fifty-three and in the prime of life. He'd be back home in a few hours with a heart prescription and doctors' orders to take it easy.

Instead my mother and brothers and sisters and I gathered in the emergency room of the Bryn Mawr Hospital and listened to a doctor softly say, "I'm sorry. We did all we could." My father was dead. My hero was gone. At age forty, his wife was a widow with seven children between ages eight and twenty-one. Certainly I had known people who had died during my still-young life; but death was supposed to happen to *older* people, in *other* families.

Shortly after we returned home from the hospital that day, my mother found a piece of paper on my father's nightstand. He was a prolific note-taker, never without pad and pen. In my mind, I can still see in his handwriting the words from the Ninetieth Psalm: "*So teach us to number our days, that we may present to You a heart of wisdom.*"

Arthur S. DeMoss was the wisest man I knew. Now he was in heaven, less surprised by his departure, I suspect, than we were. I still miss him. He never saw me play college football. His place was vacant when I married the most wonderful girl in the world. He missed greeting his first grandchildren. When I started a business, he wasn't there to advise me—though I had more counsel from him than I realized at the time, which is a large reason for my writing this book.

Seven years after my father's death, in the spring of 1986, I was working for Rev. Jerry Falwell and attending a conference at the Opryland Hotel in Nashville. We had just settled into our rooms when a call came from home telling me that my twenty-two-year-old brother, David, had been in a car accident and was in serious condition. Jerry and I checked out, flew to Philadelphia, and drove straight to the hospital at the University of Pennsylvania.

My kid brother, a wiry go-getter with a remarkable knack for making friends, just home for the summer before his final year at Liberty University, lay comatose next to a row of blinking and beeping machines. His doctors talked with us, and our friend Rev. Falwell prayed with us. Eventually we walked out of the hospital and across the street to the hotel where we would stay for the next several days. On June 6, 1986, David Arthur DeMoss joined our father in heaven.

After my father died, I somehow believed that early death would pass over the rest of my family. Why I thought that, I don't know: actuarial tables, common odds, maybe—certainly not the Bible because, if anything, it underscores life's brevity.

As I write this, I am a handful of years from the age my father was at his death and twice my brother's age when he died. The math in my head is unavoidable. I have a wife and children. I've had the thrill and challenges of building a career. I've had adult years and all that comes with new eras in life—all things David never grew up to experience.

In the early years of the church, the apostle James wrote to Christians in a distant city, "Yet you do not know what your life will be like tomorrow. You are just a vapor that appears for a little while and then vanishes away."

What is it about human nature that we so blithely presume we will have seventy or eighty years of health and life? The Creator guarantees not another breath. In the last few years, in too short a span of months, I joined the families at our children's school in mourning the loss of Carter Martin, a second grader who died following a protracted fight with cancer. I helped lift and carry the coffin of Jeanine Allen, the young mother of my daughter's best friend since kindergarten, after a seven-year battle with cancer. Through another "premature" death, I got to know Evelyn Husband, the widow of space shuttle *Discovery* Commander Rick Husband, whose shuttle blew apart as his wife and kids waited to welcome him back to earth.

"Man's days are determined," the Old Testament figure Job says as he labors to grasp his own devastating loss and grief. "You have decreed the number of his months and have set limits he cannot exceed."

When my father died, I thought I could never ever hurt that way again. Then we lost my brother David. Since then, I have been privileged to share the sorrow of other families during loss, and I know from my marrow and tissue what is important. People are. God is. Time is—important, fleeting, priceless.

———

Winston Churchill's father died at age thirty-nine, and England's future prime minister grew up expecting also to die young. In his first autobiography, the young Churchill credited his military exploits in India, including a dramatic escape atop a moving train, and in general his fearless first decades, to his awareness of the ticking clock.

My own father's death at age fifty-three circled that age

in my mind, a red mark made darker and more certain by David's sudden death only a few years later. I'm never so lost in living that I don't hear the clock tick or have an eye on the calendar—not in a paranoid sense, but with a sense of purpose. As surely as a father's life imprints on a son, a father's early death frames how his son takes on the future . . . how he looks at the past, and why he might write a book on wisdom.

I cannot remember that my father ever wasted a minute. Not that all he did was work; he frequently played tennis or Monopoly with us, went swimming or took us to professional sporting events. He was also a great conversationalist. It's just that he didn't waste time. He didn't watch TV, and he went to bed at a reasonable hour—even with guests still in the living room. ("Turn out the lights when you leave," he would say on his way upstairs.) He rose early each day. His strong sense of purpose and life fully included time to think, plan, dream, and pray.

We all are wise to invest life's most precious commodity for the greatest return. When I die, whenever that moment comes, I hope my passing will echo the psalmist's saying "Teach me to number my days, that I may present to You a heart of wisdom"—not least because my father's life and death have shown me that it is possible.

Chapter 2

STAY UNDER THE UMBRELLA

The secret of success is constancy to purpose.
Benjamin Disraeli, Earl of Beaconsfield

Years ago in Hong Kong there lived a missionary named John who had a knack for getting things done. In a densely crowded and difficult city, that brand of talent attracts attention, particularly among American businesses salivating over the lucrative Eastern market. One day the ranking executive of a squirt gun manufacturer invited John to lunch at a well-known Hong Kong restaurant. In the posh but crowded dining room, the exec slipped $600 to the owner and was escorted with John to a prime corner table.

Napkins had barely hit laps when the executive leaned in. "John," he said "we'll pay you a salary of $200,000, provide you with a nice office, and a car and driver if you'll come work for us." Perhaps too casually for the executive's pride, John said, "I'm not interested" (thinking to himself, he said later, that he could have saved the guy $600-plus on lunch). When the businessman pressed with "How much are you making now?" John didn't hesitate. "Eight thousand dollars," he said. "But that's not the point. I'm here serving God, doing what I'm supposed to do, and I've never been happier."

At 11:00 p.m. John's phone rang. "It's all over Hong Kong that you rejected that big offer at lunch today," an agitated voice with a German accent said. "I would like to know why." The caller wouldn't take tomorrow morning for an answer, and forty minutes later, still in his pajamas, John sat across a coffee table from him. His visitor said, "Everyone at the American Chamber knows what you did. I had to hear for myself."

Telling me about this incident years later, John tried to explain why the squirt gun bid and offers like it through the years failed to entice him. "I call it 'staying under the umbrella,'" he said. "Get out from under the umbrella and you get wet. I knew my calling and purpose. I wasn't going to let money or anything else sidetrack me." John is past seventy and at the panoramic end of a lifetime of serving people in Hong Kong, Asia, Africa, and dozens of places the names of which most Americans would mispronounce on the first try. Behind him lies a trail of new children's camps, orphanages, churches, and lives forever changed.

To this day, though technically retired, John has never lost his focus. He recently spent eight weeks in China doing what he has always done—serving others. In an age of business globalization, John has had abundant opportunity to act as a point man for businesses seeking to expand into markets he knows well. He could have been rich, but he would have been unhappy.

John calls it an umbrella; I call it focus—that internal compass that keeps a person on track with his gifts, his purpose, and his goals. How rare is that compass? Consider a Bureau of Labor Statistics survey that began in 1979 and tracked baby boomers' careers over the following eighteen years. The report published in 2002 revealed how many jobs people born between 1957 and 1964 held from age eighteen to age thirty-six.

Here's what they found: in an eighteen-year span, each person had held an average of ten jobs. Seventeen percent had held fifteen or more jobs—practically a different job every year. Only 18 percent had changed employment fewer than five times.

Walt Disney used to advise people to "find a job that you like so much that you'd do it without compensation; then do it so well that people will pay you to continue." To almost anyone fifty or younger, that counsel probably seems antique.

But not to me. I feel that way about my work. When I review résumés (the majority of applicants appear to want a job, not a career), before anything else, I scan down their work history. Common wisdom says that multiple jobs bespeak versatility or ambition; but for my money, that brand of résumé sprouts red flags. Don't give me changeability, give me focus. Give me loyalty. Give me longevity. Of course bad employers exist, companies downsize, families relocate, and sometimes we learn what we like by experiencing what we don't like. In the career advice category, however, I submit that the earlier a person finds his focus and the longer he has to mature it, the more likely his success.

Switching now from individuals to organizations, how many of us have walked into offices ostensibly there to make money or serve—only to scratch the surface and find that the place has no direction, no clarity of purpose?

Mackay Envelope Company is not one of those. Harvey Mackay was twenty-five when he founded the company that lives up to its name. Now the Minneapolis-based manufacturer is worth $85 million. His five hundred employees produce twenty-three million envelopes a *day*. Mackay preaches his practices in five books, including the best-selling *Swim with the Sharks Without Being Eaten Alive*.

Several years ago, I heard Harvey Mackay address a group of public relations executives in Phoenix. Something he said that day continues to ring in my head. "Our stated mission at Mackay Envelope Company," he said, "is to be in business forever," obviously proud of its profound simplicity of it. And, I thought, *That's it!* This company's compass points to true north: stick to what you know and do it better than anyone else. No tangential products or diversification for Mackay Envelope—just better envelopes, and more of them.

Now look at a global organization that the late Peter Drucker, world-renowned management expert, has called "by far the most effective organization in the U.S." Annually, its $2 *billion* budget operates with a global workforce of nearly 3.5 million staff and volunteers. More than 30 million clients a year benefit from its mission to "preach the gospel of Jesus Christ and meet human needs in His name without discrimination." The Salvation Army was founded in 1865, in England, and exported 15 years later to the United States.

Robert A. Watson, a 44 year Salvation Army veteran— for four years its highest-ranking U.S. officer—willingly reveals his employer's success method. He says, "We still operate under the same name and offer our 'customers' the same dual 'product' of salvation and service as we did more than a century ago." (Note that of all the firms on the original Dow Jones Industrials list in 1896, only one, General Electric, is still in business.)

Watson's book about his Salvation Army years, *The Most Effective Organization in the U.S.*, makes clear that even the world's best ideas land on the Army's cutting-room floor, if they skew off-mission. "We plan strategies, launch and refine programs, recruit people, and evaluate everything we do according to how it relates to preaching the gospel of Jesus Christ and meeting human needs in His name without discrimination. It's really that simple," he writes. "If a proposal doesn't advance our twofold mission, we're not interested."

The American mentality, of course, is to glance straight to the double-underlined bottom number, and Watson has more good news. "Such a laser-like focus on mission has benefits on both the revenue and the cost sides of our operations. People trust us to do what we say we're going to do, so they contribute generously." For money raised, the Salvation Army routinely sits atop the *Chronicle of Philanthropy*'s annual ranking of nonprofit organizations. In fact, the Army typically raises twice as many dollars as runner-up organizations like the Red Cross and the YMCA.

As president of The DeMoss Group, I'm in my second job since college, in the same field as my first, and have always loved my work. Mornings I get up eager for communications, words, tackling crises, and helping to inform and shape public opinion—and for the people I work alongside. Not everyone feels that way about work, and in some cases, people can't choose what they love. I still believe that much of my pleasure comes from clarity, from fixing my sight and staying with it. This company may have started without a business plan—without a budget, even—but we've never lacked for mission or focus.

From the day our business doors swung out, The DeMoss Group has delivered one service: public relations. And to one market: Christian organizations and causes. A line drawn has two sides—ours and everyone else's. Staying on our side of the line deflects any off-course project, no matter how lucrative or well-intentioned: no fund-raising counsel, no brokering radio and television time, no video production or telemarketing. The DeMoss Group is in the public relations business; we leave other services to companies better equipped to provide them.

We once declined to pursue an enticing summer-long project promoting a major sports drink. The manufacturer approached us and the work appeared to be ours for the taking—"easy money," as they say. We debated it briefly; the project was fun. It had variety, interesting new markets and contacts . . . it just had nothing to do with our company mission.

Focus is fine to write about, and the stories in this chapter may make it look simple, even simplistic. But I know well that focus, for individuals and groups, is the exception. People who want to claim or reclaim their true north can start by examining their passions, by asking what makes their hearts leap. They can ask those who know them well. Corporations and organizations with blurred vision must invest the sweat equity to produce a brief mission statement (the briefer the statement, the harder the work), then begin a day at a time, a decision at a time, to forgo the good for the great.

Whether you're called to make twenty-three million envelopes a day or serve thirty million people a year, or raise your children, or sell a service, or build a house, or plant a yard: set your focus and stay with it. Focus is the discipline to say no to anything off-mission—and that is true freedom. John the missionary had it right: find your umbrella and stay under it.

Chapter 3

TACKLE SOMETHING SO DIFFICULT YOU'LL NEVER WANT TO DO IT AGAIN

You must do the thing you think you cannot do.
Eleanor Roosevelt

On a Monday in early June, at 7:45 a.m., Dan Pinkney, a college man, pulled his car up to a housing subdivision and gestured to me in the backseat. "There's your first house," he said. "I'll pick you up at nine tonight."

I was sixteen and whatever a salesperson is, I was not. I climbed out of the car and reached back in for a small case of books. Then I turned and placed one foot in front of the other until my body stood before an aluminum-screened front door. On the first day of summer between my junior and senior years of high school, I began three months of thirteen-hour workdays in rural Pennsylvania. Home seemed far, far away, though it was only a couple of hours' drive.

Back then, the Southwestern Company of Nashville, Tennessee, did what it still does today: it trained college students in door-to-door book sales and fanned them out to work neighborhoods across the country. My friend and sales manager, Dan, was a Southwestern veteran of six summers, an extroverted purveyor of books. Until a few weeks before, I had been a comfortable introvert with no pressure to raise money for college or anything else. But my father knew sales, he knew life, and he knew me. At his urging, here I was with Dan, selling books door-to-door.

I got to know the Southwestern system in a week of long training days, part pep rally, part classroom training, and a big part memorization and mock sales presentations. My division at Southwestern sold three products: a topical Bible, a thin set of six children's books, and a medical encyclopedia. The irresistible logic was that a home with kids or grandkids needed a medical encyclopedia or more children's reading; and almost any home could use a topical Bible.

Most Southwestern trainees came motivated by the prospects of good money. The stars would earn a thousand dollars or more per week. But my family was financially comfortable and my education was guaranteed. Many of my peers took it easy that summer or worked light jobs in the final break as high school seniors. Another mental hurdle for me was a family summer vacation on the Caribbean island of St. Croix—the last getaway, it would turn out, with my father. While the rest of the DeMosses enjoyed ocean breezes at a fine resort, I would be packing Southwestern encyclopedias and Bibles up and down hot, humid neighborhood sidewalks. Which sidewalks? We didn't know.

Southwestern sales teams received their territory assignments at the end of training and not one minute before. Even Dan had no clue to where we would spend our summer. Florida? I hoped for somewhere fun. Chicago? Out West? Late Saturday night, our team was ordered to Mechanicsburg, Pennsylvania, and in a matter of hours had loaded into Dan's car with a map, sales cases, and a few dollars. No salary, no expense advance, not even a lead on room and board. By Sunday afternoon, we had rolled into Mechanicsburg, pulled up to a gas station telephone booth (remember life before cell phones?), and called a few area churches in search of rooms for rent.

One church had a retired couple with two upstairs bedrooms, and we immediately took them. We were among the fortunate few, I learned later, to snag housing on the first day. Some of the Southwestern reps lived in temporary quarters for weeks, but regardless of sleeping arrangements, that first Monday morning, everyone was selling.

As soon as we unpacked in our new rooms, we unfolded a local map. Dan produced a highlighter and divided the neighborhoods into sales regions. Before we turned in that night, one last time, a veteran and three know-nothings rehearsed their presentations.

A typical seventy-five-hour Southwestern summer work-week got us up at 6:00 a.m. By 8:00 a.m., we were striding up driveways and sidewalks to greet new Mechanicsburg prospects. By the time 9:00 p.m. rolled around, we should be wrapping up final sales. Monday through Friday—Saturdays 8:00 a.m. to 6:00 p.m.—we aimed to knock on 80 doors a day and make thirty sales presentations. On Southwestern's 42 percent commission, one Bible sale that day would net out at $27, slightly above $2 per hour.

In the beginning, the thirteen-hour workdays were to infinity and beyond. Between houses, my feet moved at glacial speed. Lunch was *slow*, and in the standstill afternoons, I frequently checked to make sure my watch was working. I was no salesman. I was lonely and intimidated. A call to my comfort zone would have been long-distance. Yet the worst part wasn't the hours and strange surroundings—the worst was the rejection. On good days, doors closed gently. Other days they slammed shut, though eventually I came to appreciate the slammers for not wasting my time.

To this day, my mother remembers the anguish from my calls home. Several times Dad refused to put her on the phone because she was standing in the background saying, "Art, please let him come home if he wants to. Tell him he doesn't have to stay out there."

Saturday nights my colleagues and I joined some fifty other Southwestern student salespeople at a local college for meetings similar to the training-week pep rallies: sales reports, success stories, selling tips, and a speaker's long-winded challenge to bring up our numbers. Those first Saturday nights always brought a lot of familiar faces. But in a short while, something else was at work: attendance was thinning. My fellow salespeople were dumping the long hours and potential income for forty-hour workweeks with guaranteed pay.

But something was at work in me too. For one thing, I had some sales under my belt. To my surprise, the sight of *college* students throwing in the towel didn't discourage me. Just the opposite: it hardened my resolve to stick it out and even make some serious money.

Nearly thirty years later, I can still remember the Great Shift. Where once I checked my watch for Dan's arrival, now I estimated hours left against doors and potential presentations. Where I had lingered over lunch, now I was skipping it altogether. When a sympathetic family invited me to stay for dinner, I weighed a helping of casserole against the loss in selling time and a spot in the Saturday night sales rankings— and politely declined. Each day as darkness fell my eyes scanned for one last house, one last prospect, one last sale.

Before the clock ran out on the summer, my personal goal was to sell $1,000 worth of books in a single week. In my final week (with a Bible I purchased for myself), I squeaked over the top. Yessir, I could sell. In a couple of hot summer months, I'd learned to love hard work, to turn undaunted from a slammed door, to budget my time, and to speak so that people would listen.

While my family was taking in Caribbean sunsets, I was learning that customers often buy the person selling rather than the product. Let my friends cruise suburban Philly in their parents' cars; in my first summer as a licensed driver, I learned how to get my foot in the door. I even learned to take cold showers in the morning, both to wake up and to resist lingering under steamy hot water (though that discipline ended with the summer).

A dozen years later when I founded a public relations firm in a new niche, I did it with no agency experience, not even an internship. But by then the three months on the pavement of Mechanicsburg, Pennsylvania, had aged into mental rocket fuel. To this day, I have never had a harder job or better training for anything that came next.

Before the next summer, during my final year of high school, Dan asked me to recruit my own team for the coming sales season, which would add student commissions on top of my own sales income. Dan is a good salesman, but the truth is that I feared going back—it was that tough; so I passed on a second tour of bookselling.

Too bad today's security worries, gated communities, and other "advancements" discourage more door-to-door sales—

(Southwestern still averages three thousand summer student salespersons, and the average first-year student earns nearly $3,000 a month. A *USA Today* story last summer featured a 21-year-old Southwestern student, Caitlyn Fogerty, who earned $16,000 in one month and $35,000 during the previous summer)—because victory at a job I initially hated forever changed how I take on a challenge.

In one form or another, we've all been told to face the things we fear. Good advice—but that summer, for me, wasn't about taking good advice. I was too young to know that a face-off against shyness could ultimately save me from myself. I just gave in to my dad's wishes. He knew what I needed, and he loved me enough not to spare the tough stuff.

By forcing me out of my comfort zone, my father taught me that a business begins where the knuckle meets the door. On my side of the door, I learned to go ahead and do something even when I was afraid. On that side of the door, I learned that selling is fundamentally person to person. For you this might mean going back to school, taking an extended missions or humanitarian relief trip, running for public office, writing a book, or anything else that forces a stretch.

I missed seeing my father that summer. I miss him still. But though at times the summer was hard on us both, and my mother, we stuck it out. In retrospect, that summer job did for me what every father wants to do for his son: it helped me become a man.

Chapter 4

THE AMAZING POWER
OF UNDERSTATEMENT

Less is more.
Robert Browning, Andrea del Sarto

We arrived at the *Washington Post* and were led into a richly paneled boardroom where editors, reporters, columnists, and editorial executives outnumbered us five or six to one. Tuxedoed waiters served lunch while I pondered what careers had sidetracked or sunk in the kind of question-and-answer sessions about to come. Editorial board meetings are a rich forum to tell your story but never without risk.

The year was 1997. Seven years earlier, a former college football coach named Bill McCartney had founded a ministry-turned-movement called Promise Keepers. Across the United States, a succession of men's stadium meetings had touched a national nerve, leading now to an event known as "Stand in the Gap—A Sacred Assembly of Men" on the

National Mall in Washington, D.C. Before that, the force of the movement would propel McCartney into the front lines of national and international media, both to promote Stand in the Gap and to explain it.

Coach was only a few years removed from a national championship at the University of Colorado, and he was no stranger to the media firing line. But this was different. As most Americans know, the road to the National Mall in Washington, D.C., is paved with the ambitions of leaders come to flex their movement's political muscle, size, or solidarity. The power, the punch, the bragging rights, the proof, the influence . . . lie in how many people show up. The larger the crowd, the stronger the statement.

The trick—in the absence of turnstiles, fixed seating, or gate receipts—is to know how many people that is. Until Stand in the Gap, a host organization typically predicted a record-breaking attendance. Then at the actual event the National Park Police released an official crowd estimate— invariably *below* the group's predictions and hopes—and the group would immediately charge the Park Police with bias.

That day in the *Post* boardroom, the crowd estimate question came early: "So, Coach, how many people are you expecting?" As Promise Keepers' spokesperson, I fielded that one. I said, "We won't *project* a number ahead of time, *estimate* a number on that day, or *debate* your number the following day." The journalists looked at us. I put it another way: "We expect a lot of men. But we have no idea how many." To forgo predicting attendance was obviously atypical.

As it happened, the same year that Promise Keepers assembled on the National Mall, the National Park Service had stopped issuing crowd estimates. That suited us fine. In the place where groups traditionally gathered for a show of power, Promise Keepers would show humility. "You'll see no political speeches," we told the *Post*. "No attempts to influence legislation. No local or national dignitaries—elected or unelected—seated on the platform. No signed petitions and no signs with slogans."

From that moment, our strength would not be numbers, but images—scenes of men committed to What Matters. Weeks earlier, one of Bill's staff members had located a Washington-based aerial photography company. For a fee, their photos would download instantly into a computer program that rendered precise crowd figures. But we advised against the service, even for internal records. "If the crowd is small, we won't *want* an official number," I proposed. "If the crowd is large, we won't *need* it."

The Saturday in October finally arrived and so did the men. From just after midnight until the official start at 10:00 a.m., buses streamed into Washington, D.C. We issued media credentials to 1,098 reporters from around the globe. C-SPAN aired the entire event live to some 90 million homes. Before a watching world, men from across America and from several dozen other nations filled the National Mall from the Capitol steps all the way to the Washington Monument. On either side the crowd spilled at least two blocks onto side streets and into adjoining neighborhoods. Independently, various media organizations that day estimated a million men; Stand in the Gap was termed one of the largest gatherings ever held in the nation's capital.

By the end of the event, our decision to pump the brakes on hyperbole had two important effects. First, the journalists who covered Stand in the Gap had nothing to challenge, nothing to attack, and no basis on which to label it less than successful. Second, images had said more, and with greater impact, than any boast beforehand could have.

"*Under-promise, over-deliver,*" we say at our firm, and so we advise our clients. A decade later, I still believe a significant part of the "Stand in the Gap" success was our determined and public focus on why we came, and not on how many came with us. To this day I believe we earned the media's respect by forgoing the numbers game.

I have yet to see the company fail that promises less and delivers more. On the other hand, I have a bulging file of examples to prove that bold predictions can snatch defeat out of the jaws of victory. Too many times a leader or spokesperson publicly projects, say, sixty thousand attendees, only to have twenty thousand actually appear. The shame is that an audience of twenty thousand people for almost any occasion is hardly small. But relative to the advance pronouncement—well, they've set themselves up to fail.

Some years after Promise Keepers' successful day in Washington, another religious event was held on the National Mall. The *Washington Post* printed reports from the event's organizers projecting a crowd of one hundred thousand, based on two years of planning and strong local support (and a history of drawing large crowds from around the world). Opening night, however, drew only ten thousand people—still no small feat given the cool October temperatures and heavy driving rains that soaked the nation's capital. But the rain couldn't take all the blame for the letdown—much of it belonged to predicting a crowd ten times the size of the one that showed up.

Some years ago, an international religious leader set up a charity in Africa to save a million orphans of the AIDS epidemic. He began to mobilize people and resources to house thousands of children—a significant start, no doubt. Plans were under way to build an industrial park and an entire educational system on thousands of acres. The nation took notice, wondering, perhaps, if it might be too good to be true.

Before one shovel of dirt was turned, the head of the charity publicly announced that the project would be "the largest humanitarian religious movement in the history of the world from the U.S. to Africa." Four months later, still before ground had been broken, the same man resigned from the charity and left the continent, leaving a new president and a bewildered staff to make good on his promise. "I'll put it down as one of the disappointments of my career," he later said.

In this case, and in this beleaguered country, a project a fraction of the size and scope of what had been announced would have been among the most expansive charitable programs in that nation's history. In fact, this man's work had already accomplished great things in a few short years. Thousands of Christian volunteers, for example, had responded to his call for help and traveled to this country to plant hundreds of thousands of vegetable gardens, serving impoverished families who could now grow their own food.

Such tangible programs would stand even taller if not for a premature announcement of the "largest humanitarian religious movement in the history of the world from the U.S. to Africa." Minus that public declaration, the project would have wildly exceeded expectations and genuinely lifted spirits. Instead, spirits, hopes, and dreams were needlessly dashed.

Unfortunately (though sometimes deservedly), my field of PR often gets tagged with slurs like *spin*, *puff*, or *hype*. On the Web, I actually discovered a firm called Hype Public Relations, that claimed "unparalleled success in establishing credibility and brand awareness for its clients." I thought to myself: *What companies hand their credibility to a firm called Hype? Webster's* says *hype* means "deceit." Flip ahead to *hyperbole*, and you get "figurative language that greatly overstates or exaggerates facts." Hardly the calling card I would look for.

Our firm is "anti-hype"—sometimes to our own detriment when people are seeking (and will pay for) hard sell on soft evidence. But a group or project that would fail to justify notice on its own merit, minus the hype, would not want us working for them. And we say so.

Once at an introductory meeting with a relatively new client, we were laying out this public relations philosophy when the client interrupted. "You have an opportunity to change our view of public relations firms," he told us. That was music to my ears. Evidently his past experience involved public relations firms promising the moon but delivering moon pies.

After years of brushing up against all kinds of people in the public eye, I've learned that great leaders are first of all great servants—and that great service is modest, understated, in speech and action. Understatement is self-restraint, and self-restraint is hardly a sign of weakness. On the contrary, wisely used, few things carry more power.

Chapter 5

WORK LESS, THINK MORE

The significant problems we face in life cannot be
solved at the same level of thinking we were at
when we created them.
Albert Einstein

Companies pay $450,000 and up for Joey Reiman's big ideas, some of which take him only a month to produce. One CEO, Jim Adamson of the Advantica Restaurant Group, proudly boasts, "I paid Joey Reiman $1 million just to think!" Joey, erstwhile ad agency owner, heads BrightHouse, "the world's first ideation corporation." His autobiography of adventures into both sides of his brain, appropriately titled *Thinking for a Living*, was a gift to me from one of my associates on our company's seventh anniversary.

And the book? After browsing just one chapter, I ordered copies for every member of our staff and made it required reading. Then I scheduled an off-site session for all of us to explore, individually and as a firm, how to improve our thinking. I remember my children's surprise that morning at breakfast when I told them the firm was shutting down operations to talk about *thinking*. (Regretably, this announcement would puzzle many adults too.)

Joey Reiman's passion for good thinking and his six-to-seven-figure fees for doing it definitely had my attention. On the last page of his book, Reiman invites his readers to write him personally; so I wrote that not only was I challenged, but I had purchased his book for every employee of my public relations firm (sufficient flattery for most authors), and I wanted him to speak to us at a "thinking lunch."

A few days later Joey Reiman's office called and said yes to lunch. We paid Joey around $1,500; and though we were fortunate to tap his mind, the wonder that day was his enthusiasm for thinking, something I preached around our shop since day one. As he closed, Joey invited any of us to drop by the BrightHouse headquarters in Atlanta; but first he warned us. "You won't find people hustling and bustling around," he said. "They'll be sitting in their offices with their feet propped on the desk, *thinking*." And we heard again about his half-million-dollar fees.

Well, Joey Reiman *was* entertaining and motivating, but hundreds of thousands for a month of work? Marketing sizzle, I thought. A little hype, perhaps. Five years later, I was having lunch with an executive of a major corporation in the

31

Southeast when Joey's name came up. Turns out, my lunch companion's company was well into a BrightHouse month of thinking.

I said, "I need to ask you something."

Without waiting to hear my question, he said, "It's true."

"The fee?" I asked.

"The fee," he said. "Half a million dollars. We're paying it." And he said it as if they'd snagged a bargain.

The corporate world is naturally tilted toward furious doers rather than great thinkers. Everyone, it seems, is busy designing, writing, building, producing, implementing— unfortunately, too much of it is divorced from good *thinking*. So we continue to design, write, build, produce, and implement . . . doing business as usual.

The business of public relations requires considerable doing, but I determined long ago to distinguish our firm for thinking. Anyone can issue a news release, schedule a press conference, or buy an ad. A thinking PR professional might do those things, or something altogether different.

Part of the problem is that thinking looks so suspiciously like resting. Lest anyone see a BrightHouse professional tilted back in her desk chair, feet up, and conclude that her hard work is time off, think again. Henry Ford called thinking "the hardest work there is, which is probably why so few engage in it." Joey Reiman said that when people hear what he does for a living, they usually have two responses: "Wow, what's a

32

thinker?" followed closely by "What does a thinker think about?" To which Joey answers: "A thinker thinks about everything."

Where *are* the thinkers? I'd say they're bottlenecked behind two big challenges. First is the time and quiet that good thinking requires. The rest of the world crams our mental space with television, radio, iPods, BlackBerries, books, magazines, meetings, e-mail, video games, and the Internet. Good thinking isn't one more task of a multitasker; it needs its own time. So the question becomes how to get the time and space.

One suggestion would be to turn off the car radio or CD player, at least some of the time. Another might be to exercise without television or music—just you and the birds, or just you and the treadmill motor. On that day, you will think for thirty minutes more than most exercisers.

Warren Buffett is universally revered as the world's greatest investor, and is one of the richest men alive. He heads Berkshire Hathaway, a $136 billion investment firm, and is personally worth some $43 billion. Maybe you're picturing him in a Wall Street penthouse, but Mr. Buffett was born in Omaha, Nebraska, and never left. "You can think here," he said. "You can think better about the market; you don't hear so many stories, and you can just sit and look at the stock on the desk in front of you. You can think about a lot of things." This comes from a man whose company stock trades at more than $100,000 per share.

Here's another idea: eat lunch alone at least a couple of times a week. I dine alone probably four of every five business days not because I'm a quiet guy, but to think—or to read and think, or to write and think, or to plan and think.

While working on this book, I visited a Barnes & Noble bookstore where a business title jumped off the shelf: *Never Eat Alone, and Other Secrets to Success, One Relationship at a Time*. The premise is that every minute is ripe for networking, schmoozing, trading business cards, connecting, and following up. No, some minutes are ripe for thinking . . . *alone*. And be honest—more often than not, restaurant patrons and much of the business crowd are colleagues socializing. Not to take away from the benefits of human contact, but if thinking is a priority, you can deliberately and more frequently also lunch alone.

A second challenge to good thinking is that too few people and organizations value or demand it. Most people are busy doing what they've always done. As if bosses and clients believe motion alone justifies a paycheck, busyness becomes its own end. But precede that work with deliberate thinking (maybe even some feet-on-the-desk time), and the result might take you somewhere completely different, even better.

Joey Reiman distinguishes great thinkers from others this way: "Great thinkers think *inductively*, that is, they create the solution and seek out the problems that the solution might solve; most companies think *deductively*, that is, defining a problem and then investigating different solutions."

U.S. News & World Report recently ranked *New York Times* columnist Thomas Friedman among "America's best leaders." Friedman, whose column appears in seven hundred newspapers worldwide, was praised for his "rarefied position in journalism, several rungs above a talking head or policy wonk." Friedman, the magazine said, is an "influential thinker." What a compliment.

For a guy with no PR background (no school courses in public relations, communications, or journalism), I confess that at the beginning, in the news release and press conference fundamentals, my firm was average at best. Our unique selling feature was the think factor. What we may have lacked in form on the front end, we supplied in a well-thought-out reason for what we did.

That practice is far from new, and has impressive pedigree. In 1501 when the Arte della Lana commissioned Michelangelo to create a statue of David, they gave him the same block of marble that Agostino di Duccio had unsuccessfully tried to sculpt some forty years earlier. The story is told that every day for three months, the twenty-six-year-old Michelangelo stood and stared at the marble block. He would leave at the end of the workday and return the following morning, repeating the routine to the great puzzlement of onlookers.

"What are you doing?" someone asked.

"I'm working," the master sculptor replied.

Think about it.

Chapter 6

BUY SOME STAMPS

To send a letter is a good way to move somewhere
without moving anything but your heart.
Phyllis Theroux

Check your mailbox. If you're an average American, you'll have to receive 100 pieces of mail if you're hoping to get just one personal letter. What's more, that personal mail is most likely not a letter at all, but a greeting card, an announcement, or an invitation.

What the postal service calls "household-to-household" correspondence is less than 1 percent of the 100 billion pieces of first-class mail every year. The quickest blame goes to e-mail, but I suspect that letter writing began its regrettable decline with the lowered cost of long-distance phone calls. For whatever reason, people no longer reach out and touch through thoughtful, lasting, handwritten (or even typed) words on paper. And I mourn the loss.

I mourn it, and I resist it. On a recent flight from New York to Atlanta, I wrote five letters. Driving home from the airport, I dictated three more. E-mail and cell phones have their places, but for human expression that survives long after digital impulses disappear in the ether, I invest the time and money to write and send real mail.

Not long ago in the *New York Times*, James Fallows, a national correspondent for the *Atlantic Monthly*, mourned the nearly extinct pleasure of receiving what someone took the time to write, fold, seal, and mail. "To leaf through a box of old paper correspondence is to know what has been lost in the shift," Fallows wrote. "The pretty stamps, the varying look and feel of handwritten and typed correspondence, the tangible object that was once in the sender's hands."

Personal letters are tangible history writ small—loves, little milestones, and otherwise forgotten news of nations, soldiers, friends, scientists, statesmen, sweethearts . . . and our family members. Collected letters of Ronald Reagan or George Bush and others break the great men and women into the sums of their relationships, days, observations, thoughts, personalities, and reactions. A letter worth keeping takes us back to a time when thoughts were worth shaping—a time when people and words deserved our best effort.

When the United States Postal Service published a "Mail Moment" survey, it concluded with the bittersweet observation that "two-thirds of all consumers do not expect to receive personal mail, but when they do, it makes their day. This hope keeps them coming back each day." The survey said that 55 percent of Americans look forward to the possibilities in each day's mail. So why do we keep disappointing them?

Among the letters that still lift me is one from my father dated June 19, 1979—the summer I left home to sell books door-to-door. Seventy-four days later my father would die of a heart attack. But on that day, June 19, he was thinking of me, and he wrote on his beautiful National Liberty Corporation letterhead:

Dear Mark:

It was good chatting with you last night, and I'm glad to see how enthused you are about what you will be doing this summer.

Again, I am confident this will prove to be a great and wonderfully worthwhile experience, regardless of how little or much money you earn. As you indicated, the discipline itself will be excellent and I am sure the experience will prove to be invaluable in whatever you decide to do with your life.

We really miss you already! Selfishly, we wish you were here with us. But I know this is going to be in your best

interest. I am praying especially for these first few days during this time of getting acclimated, after which I feel sure the whole thing will become much easier.
With much love,
Dad

P.S. I want you to know—I'm very proud of you!

That was my mail moment. The letter is typed, but the P.S. was in my dad's familiar hand. A quarter century later, this last-ever letter from him is a physical piece of his thoughts with me; 160 words of love and encouragement with his valuable perspective on money, empathy, and his belief in me, brimming with pride.

In 1989, my sister was working in the United States Senate for Jesse Helms of North Carolina. She must have told the senator about the birth of our first child because he took the time to write to us. To this day, I love that letter:

Dear Mark and April:

Dorothy and I have been so excited about the arrival of Georgia Ann, and want to meet that young lady at the first opportunity. Since she'll be three months old next week, I wonder how much she weighs now.

While I know there's no shortage of Bibles and New Testaments in your home, perhaps you'll want to put the enclosure in a drawer so, some years hence, Georgia Ann will know that there was an old Senator who loved her even before he met her.

I hope you three are doing well, and we send our affectionate best wishes to you.

God bless you always.

Sincerely,

Jesse

Eighteen months later, another envelope from the United States Senate appeared in our mailbox:

Dear Mark and April—and Georgia!

There was a real angel gracing your lovely Christmas card this year—but I cannot believe Georgia has already become a captivating young lady. She is gorgeous.

Right after the election, I had to come right back here to participate in the Ethics Committee hearings—which just seem to go on and on, and on and on. I do so much want to be home with the children and grandchildren, instead of being here.

You have brightened my day, and I am so deeply grateful.

Several times during past years, I have sent special friends the text of a Christmas prayer delivered in the Senate more than 50 years ago by Dr. Peter Marshall. I have been pleasantly surprised that many friends have asked me to do that again this year.

Thank you for your friendship, and best wishes for a joyful and meaningful Holy season—and a Happy New Year! Sincerely,

Jesse

At the time, we lived in Virginia and could not vote for this senator. How many people he must have written during his thirty-year Senate career, I cannot know. But on the theory that people tend to behave consistently, I bet more than a few folks still have valued missives from this man they admired. A few years after hearing from Senator Helms, April and I took our sweet Georgia to Washington and introduced her to him in his office—a man as gracious in person as on paper.

Where letter writing is practiced, some letters leave indelible prints on hearts and souls. Golf great Phil Mickelson tells the story of his 2004 Masters' win—his first "major"—in a book titled *One Magical Sunday*. Critics and pundits had long maintained that Mickelson's aggressive style of play had prevented him from winning a major—though he had already won many PGA tournaments. As he reflected on his history-making moment in sports, he recalled . . . a letter:

> It was an exceptional day. In particular, it was very meaningful for me to win the Masters' during Arnold Palmer's final competitive appearance here. I couldn't help but think back to the letter he wrote to me after the 2002 Bay Hill Invitational. "You never would have won as many tournaments as you have by playing a more conservative game," he wrote. "Keep playing to win. Keep charging. Your majors will come."

A letter's impact almost always exceeds the writer's effort. Once when the sister of a friend of mine was in prison, I took five minutes to write to her parents that I was praying for them. Within a day, my friend had e-mailed me: her dad had called her about the "wonderful, handwritten letter." The timing was impeccable, she said. Her parents were feeling so alone. The next time my friend's father visited her he brought my note to show her.

My love of letter writing turns on wheels large and small.

I love to order personalized stationery in sizes to cover any occasion or letter length. I love to survey and purchase postage stamps. I loved the Ronald Reagan commemorative stamps and bought up some of the first issues. If Reagan doesn't appeal to you, you can express yourself with stamps of Greta Garbo, Cesar Chavez, Henry Fonda, Arthur Ashe, Lewis & Clark, fish, cartoons, clouds, lizards, flowers . . . .

My wife and I both come from solid letter-writing stock. Before my father-in-law retired as president of A. L. Williams Insurance Company, he signed hundreds of letters every morning to individual members of his sales force—to people he wished to single out for recognition and encouragement. To most letters, he added a handwritten note. He remains a prolific letter writer, continuing to make prolific letter savers of the rest of us: his children, grandchildren, and friends across the country.

What I am trying to say is that words matter, and the words we take time to commit to paper matter even more—and occasions to write them abound. For example, in one recent span I wrote:

➣ A family of two girls and a dad who lost their mom and wife to cancer—to assure them of my love and continued prayers. Having lost my father and a brother at young ages, perhaps my letter connected with them during their grief.

➤ An employee's spouse who lost his job—to encourage him and offer any help I could give in his search.

➤ The fiancée of one of our employees—to welcome her to our "company family."

➤ The basketball coach at the high school I graduated from (I didn't even play for him but was a classmate and football teammate of his son's)—to commend him on a championship season and for staying at the same school for so long.

➤ My sophomore high school history teacher (I never liked history, but I liked and admired *him*)—thanking him for staying at that school nearly thirty years.

➤ The speaker I brought in for our company retreat—just to thank him. (He told me that nearly half of our staff had also written to thank him and that he put these letters in his "encouragement file.")

➤ A pastor friend in Florida—congratulating him on the publication of his first book, which I had discovered in the San Francisco airport and read on my flight home.

➤ Every employee, on the occasion of our company Christmas party—to thank them for working with me. Invariably, many will say the personal note is more meaningful than the profit-sharing check that accompanies it.

➤ Friends on the West Coast who lost a child to leukemia—to encourage them and grieve with them.

➤ The parents of a college intern who spent the summer working in our office—to tell them what a fine daughter they had raised.

➤ A columnist in a national magazine—to thank him for a particularly meaningful column in which he shared some very personal trials he was enduring.

➤ A high school basketball teammate of my daughter's—to encourage her during a period I knew she was discouraged about her playing time. At the next game her father thanked me, saying, "You will never know how much your letter meant to her; she needed that."

Now, could I have said these same things in e-mails? The answer lies in a second question: would it have meant as much?

Letter writing is a wonderful personal practice, but it's also good business: successful professionals generally are good letter writers. I once wrote three executives from the same company, including the chairman of the board. The only one who wrote back was the most successful of all, and the busiest—the chairman.

That same week I wrote letters to two coaches—a high school coach, and Mark Richt, head football coach at the University of Georgia. Coach Richt wrote back within days, and during a crucial part of his season. The other coach did not. Again, successful people, no matter how busy, seem to make time to write letters.

Late one evening I went to kiss my sixteen-year-old daughter good night after what seemed to have been a tough day for her. I found her sitting on her bed flipping through a box of papers.

"What's that?" I said.

"It's my letterbox," she said.

I hadn't known she had a letterbox. But from over her shoulder I saw one of my notes, and I smiled.

Chapter 7

TECHNOLOGY ISN'T EVERYTHING

Technology has kind of turned the tables on us.
We move to its speed and its rhythm.
Carl Honore

One day at the DeMoss home our high-speed Internet service lost its zip and we had the good fortune to retain a service technician. The nice man that came to our home set a mystical meter on the box where the street cable connected to our house, and he waited a few minutes. "Ah," he said after a while in a friendly voice. "Not enough juice coming through this line. No wonder you're getting slow Internet." With a few adjustments, he pronounced us in good shape, packed up his meter box and drove into the night.

Back in the house, however, our Internet speed was unchanged. The next morning I dialed, er, *punched* in the cable company telephone number—an office only two miles away—to schedule a quick and easy return visit.

Welcome to Cable Communications. For quality assurance purposes, your call may be monitored. Please enter your ten-digit phone number.

So far, so good. I knew my phone number.

To make a payment on your account, or for account balance information, press "1."

To order new service or to add additional service, press "2."

If you are experiencing technical difficulties with any of our products, press "3."

For billing questions, press "4."

To disconnect or remove service, press "5."

I paused to consider the options.

If you'd like to hear this menu again, press "9."

No number exactly matched my situation, so I pressed "9," hoping to reach the nice fellow from the night before. After listening a second time to my five options, I pressed "3."

If you would like to confirm a previously scheduled appointment, press "1."

No . . . no need to *confirm* a previously scheduled appointment. I needed to *discuss* an appointment that actually occurred the previous evening. I listened further.

To reset your converter box, press "2."

No converter box at our house.

For cable TV support, press "3." For high-speed Internet support, press "4."

Every well-intentioned press of a new number on the

dial pad drove me further from my simple request. A disembodied but chipper female voice directed me to a Web site if I preferred that method. Wasn't bad Web reception my presenting problem? The voice offered me every option but the reasonable purpose for my call. Then came the words I longed for: *to speak with a customer service representative, please press zero.* I pressed zero, but still no human voice came, and now late for the office, I gave up.

On the way out the door, I groused to my wife about the quagmire, and she offered to pick up where I left off. "No," I said. "I'll drop by their office and do it in person."

She turned and looked at me. "Don't waste your time," she said. "I've tried that before. That's not a real office. They just refer you to their toll-free number or Web site. No customer service people work there."

And so it goes in homes across the nation and the American pursuit of help for our mostly service-free technology. We love what technology does when it works. When it breaks down, we're talking to ourselves. Two-thirds of customers who try to get service online, says a survey by Gartner Research, a technology consultancy, finally quit and try to use the telephone.

But turning to telephone voice menus is like going from a bad car to a broken unicycle. Fourteen of fifteen voice-response systems, according to Forrester Research, earn failing grades. Another study says that three-quarters of people calling for help with technology problems eventually dissolve into "customer rage."

Companies everywhere seem eager to address customer frustration. How? Why, with improved technology! Still another study (frustration draws studies, if nothing else) found that 37 percent of callers to automated systems immediately press zero hoping to speak with a human. One creative blogger launched an online customer-service "cheat sheet" with tricks to reach a live operator at frequently called companies.

All of this is a lot of trouble. And it comes to us compliments of not just large corporations but comparatively small businesses and groups lured by the siren call of "cost-effective customer service." Several friends whom I periodically telephone, pastors of large churches, to be fair, are caught in the same technology trap as the most "progressive" corporations when it comes to fielding phone calls.

To give the automated phone-answering system its due, a programmed black box can take and route your message. If your problem or need fits snugly into one of half a dozen options, it can send you blithely to the next level of digital delay. But for all the miracles of ones and zeros, a machine cannot hear urgency in my voice. An electronic impulse cannot poke its head down the hall to tell me the pastor's assistant is only at the copying machine—or about to wrap up the call she's on now. No sensor can inform me that the associate actually is in the pastor's office and both are expecting my call. So though we all might have been available to talk, we may not connect now for several hours, or even days.

This is precisely why a caller to The DeMoss Group has only two routes into company voice mail: call at night, or specifically request someone's voice mail. Between 8:30 a.m. and 6:00 p.m., callers to our office, without fail, encounter a human being with a pleasant voice. Sherry or Brenda or Gillian know where to find the person you're calling, what calls are expected, when we left the office, when our flight lands, and so on.

If I'm unavailable, our real-live phone answerers will connect you with a colleague no doubt able to help you just as well—something even the most sophisticated voice mail system cannot do. The DeMoss Group will not transfer callers into the great digital abyss. And when holograms replace receptionists, we will cling resolutely to the hopelessly Dark Age of live operators.

And now to e-mail—one giant leap for mankind and one giant step backward for the human arts of thinking, conversing, and spending personal time with other people. In 2002, human beings used technology to send and receive 400,000 terabytes of information by e-mail. How much is that? The print equivalent of 40 *thousand* Libraries of Congress. Consider first the power of an incoming e-mail to rip its recipient from a project, her focus on a phone conversation, or any one of a list of more personal activities.

Think about it. Please. When a letter arrives by way of the U.S. Postal Service, do you immediately open it and sit down to reply? When an overnight letter delivered by FedEx lands on your desk, do you answer it that very moment by return FedEx? Where is it written that an electronic message must be answered at corresponding speed?

While we sit at our desks ravaging our eyesight on the screens before us, e-mail more tightly enslaves a nation's workforce. Rarely can I walk the length of our office hallway without someone asking whether I read the e-mail sent to me only moments earlier. Rarely do I answer yes.

I am convinced that the majority of men and women pull into their parking spaces every weekday morning fully intending to turn out a day's work, only to leave eight or nine hours later with no achievement beyond answered e-mail. It is possible to pass a career and a life planted before a computer screen like Pavlov's dog, answering e-mail and hitting Send, answering e-mail and hitting Send, answering e-mail and hitting Send, answering e-mail and hitting Send.

This picture so disturbs me that I intentionally spend hours of my weekday beyond the reach of my computer, working at a table or on a sofa away from my desk. I need the concentrated non-illuminated-screen time to practice what an entire generation is forgetting how to do (and a new generation is likely never to learn): to think and read and discuss and write.

Warren Buffett runs a multibillion-dollar investment firm and is America's second richest man, behind Bill Gates. He also spends most of his day in an office with no computer. Well, you say, he must spend his day attached to a phone talking to people attached to computers. Wrong. A *Wall Street Journal* reporter who profiled Buffett wrote that on a recent weekday he received but thirteen phone calls, including one wrong number.

Now, while I resist technology's robotization of human workers, I am far from being antitechnology. Our firm recently paid an industry expert $10,000 to spend one day teaching us the effective use of blogs. I own a BlackBerry (more accurately, a Palm Treo), as do several of our staff members who travel significantly.

Our office is wireless, and we purchase new computer equipment every several years. We regularly upgrade server speed and capacity to maintain every possible communications edge, and we just installed the latest, greatest phone system we could find. But aided by those digital advances, I want a culture of workers able to think, speak, plan, and write—pursuits that, done well, require time uninterrupted.

The issue, therefore, is not technology vs. no technology,

but how to use it wisely and well. As a guideline, I suggest that *we*, and not the technology or corporations that develop it, make the rules. I will decide when I read your e-mail and when I answer it. My response to you, while timely, will not necessarily match the speed of instant messaging that so enamors our kids.

Second, I will use technology when and where it helps, and otherwise ignore it, unplug it, walk away from it, turn it off—whatever it takes. I own a Palm Treo not so I can read your e-mail as I walk down the hall of my office to the restroom. I have it so I can get your e-mail while riding in a taxicab in Los Angeles or waiting in an airport lounge for my delayed flight home.

Consequently, I may go days, even a week or more, without turning it on. And I *sure* don't wear it on my belt so it can send a shock to my waist every time a new message (or piece of spam) arrives. "The art of being wise," wrote nineteenth-century philosopher William James, "is the art of knowing what to overlook."

Finally, I am determined to be where I am—in the room and in the present. Technology has crippled civility and cordiality. Of ten people at a boardroom table, six or seven may simultaneously be in other cybermeetings, thumbs glued to BlackBerries, oblivious to the person speaking or presenting at the head of the table. A nation's workforce increasingly aids and abets corporate robbery as technology relieves us of our solitude and space, our minds and our thinking, our real presence with sons and daughters, spouses and parents.

And as it turns out, with all our advancements, life has no rewind.

Chapter 8

HONESTY CAN BE COSTLY

Honesty's the best policy.
Miguel de Cervantes, *Don Quixote*

I n the fourth quarter, as if capping an already record year, our biggest client signed a new contract with us at three times our largest fee ever. I know . . . Business 101 warns not to let a single client be too big a piece of the pie. But there we were, one client—one signed contract—now a full third of our company's annual income.

Two weeks into the new contract year, my vice president and I put final touches on a comprehensive plan to lift our client to new levels of public awareness. The pieces of the plan fit and turned like interlocking gears: media relations, events, message points, collateral materials, and crisis management. We slid the documents into our briefcases and flew to meet with the client.

Picture now a small conference room and the long hand

on my watch crawling to our three o'clock meeting. The one person missing was the vice president who had awarded us the ambitious contract. Running late, I mused, just about the time the communications director slid something across the table.

"I've been instructed to go ahead and start the meeting," he said. "Why don't you begin by reading this?"

I opened the envelope and felt the color leave my face. The man across the table had never supported our role. His letter called for a significantly reduced agreement.

The issue behind this silent drama was not budgetary but a clash of public relations philosophies. Years later, I can still remember the premise of that letter: our client clearly resented the idea that we believed we knew better than they what their public relations program should be like. The letter suggested that my company continue to write and distribute the organization's news releases and press kits, but public relations counsel would no longer be sought or paid for.

The letter lay before me. "Your organization took forty-five days to respond to our contract," I said. "I'm not going to respond to this letter in a forty-five-minute meeting. Let's just adjourn until your vice president can join us."

After a while, the vice president did come in, and though he brought no immediate consolation, more of the fog burned off. Yes, he had increased our responsibility and compensation. Yes, he had signed a contract. But their director of communications now wished to reverse the decision, and he had permitted it.

Time seemed to stand still between that afternoon's body slam and the late-night flight home. My colleague and I spent the hours deliberating in an airport lounge. Our most obvious response would be to restructure along the client's direction and salvage a big part of the billings. But both of us were still stunned and too fatigued to decide anything. We'd talk more the next day.

With the dawn came my answer. I would resign the entire account. We are a public relations firm, not a news release factory. We would not separate thinking from doing. And while this was our truest option, I knew it would affect every employee. I talked it over with my three senior advisers, who supported my decision, and we called together the entire staff. Telling the story never got easy. I choked up as I told them they deserved better from this client.

The resignation letter we sent burned no bridges (they rehired us a couple of years later), though I did plead guilty to the charge that we acted as if we knew what they needed better than they did. That's usually why clients hire us. Our issue now, as we saw it, was whether to take a check at any cost, and we would not. Not even our biggest check ever to that point. Only time would show us that the high-stakes break made us a better company and me a stronger leader.

One thing about public relations is that ultimately a client pays for intangibles. Our stock amounts to relationships, time, experience, knowledge, creativity, ideas . . . objective counsel. And while every project may have some standard early steps, the outcome is never a given, never a promise, never a formula. Mix in the fact that not every person or group has a true read on its own newsworthiness or public perception, and you begin to understand the potential gap between a seasoned PR perspective and a client's own wishes or hopes.

We built our practice by telling clients what they *need* to hear—the truth—not necessarily what they *want* to hear. In our business it's easy to say, "Sure, we think we can get you on *Larry King Live* or in the *New York Times*." Or, "We think your book is the best we've seen this year, and we'll pitch it to every major media outlet in the country." But easy isn't always right.

When that gap between wishes and truth is severe, a public relations firm has three options. First and easiest is to charge for what *might* happen and start the clock. Second is to counsel the client to change in ways that will move it closer to its goals. Third is to tell the client or candidate that unless you've got the goods, no firm can get you on the five o'clock news or *Oprah*, at which point you decline the work or the client declines you.

Some years ago, one of our clients wrote what he believed to be one of that year's landmark books. His publisher offered us first shot to promote it and sent us the book manuscript with a memo. They expected to appear on *Today, Good Morning America,* in the *New York Times* Book Review section . . . and in other prominent national media outlets.

But the book had no mainstream news value. Unwilling to waste my client's money or jeopardize our credibility with media, I believe I surprised the publisher by telling him their ambitions were unrealistic and we could not meet them. Not surprisingly, within a week, another firm signed to publicize the project, though high-level coverage never came.

Over the years, our work philosophy has cost us existing business, kept us from winning new business, *and* gotten us fired (among many successful projects, I should add). A national youth organization, already a client of ours for several years, wanted to appeal more directly to teen audiences and asked us to help them with a re-branding effort. Their new brand, we said, must leap into the contemporary young person's mind. The group needed to be more ESPN than C-SPAN. But this group was long-standing and our suggestions were apparently too disruptive to the status quo. Within a month of our presentation to their board they fired us, costing us significant money for work already done.

Another time, an up-and-coming pastor of a large, growing church flew in to see me. Our discussion of public relations included questions about lifestyle issues, such as the appropriateness of his buying a Rolls-Royce (which I could not endorse). He had arrived ready to write a first month's retainer check. I suggested he wait for a proposal, which I sent a week later. I never heard from him again.

On another occasion, a large, national Christian nonprofit organization wanted a public relations firm to help manage a crisis. On a conference call with several leaders of the ministry, I advised of the importance of financial disclosure, evidently something they did not practice. They requested a face-to-face meeting at their headquarters and we set a date. My assistant later received a call informing us the meeting would have to be postponed, and we heard from them no more.

The money we've lost in business declined would tally into hundreds of thousands of dollars, no small thing for an agency our size; but I've never regretted the lines we've drawn. I've never regretted not compromising what we know to tell people what they might want to hear. Even when it comes at a high cost, honesty is always a bargain.

Chapter 9

GOOD PEOPLE ARE EVERYTHING; MONEY ISN'T

*You can buy a person's hands but you can't
buy his heart. His heart is where
his enthusiasm is, his loyalty is.*
Stephen Covey

The idea came to me seven years ago, but I remember as if it were yesterday the mental conflict that came with it. I was the young president of a relatively new firm with the uncommon idea to reward good work with no work at all. As my valuable vice president's first five-year mark approached, I wondered if it wouldn't be wise to preempt any burnout by giving her paid leave—a sabbatical—then making that five-year reward standard company policy.

The dissenter in my head ended every sentence with a question mark. Could a company of eight or ten people afford in workload alone to give up a key person, even for a few weeks? What about clients who relied on her service and counsel? What if, during her time away, she decided to change companies or careers? What if more and more employees began to qualify? (I now believe one of the indicators of the strength of our firm is how many people have taken sabbaticals.) What then? Few companies offer that kind of time off—maybe for good reason.

I told myself that the risks of underwriting a sabbatical fall far below the risk of a valued employee feeling wrung out and unappreciated. Furthermore, if one person's absence can jeopardize an entire operation, we had bigger problems than time off. I also thought of the pleasure of telling a faithful worker to wrap up five years of effort by refueling her personal interests, then coming back to us. Someone who found herself renewed after the first five years, I reasoned, was more likely to stay a second five.

So with some fanfare, I introduced The DeMoss Group sabbatical. After five years of service, any employee of any rank (companies that offer sabbaticals typically limit them to executives) was entitled to four consecutive weeks of paid leave—with the option to attach another week of regular vacation. We also would reimburse up to $2,500 in travel expenses.

To show that The DeMoss Group meant business, anyone on sabbatical would be fully extracted from all firm work. No checking e-mail or voice mail. No calls, for any reason, from fellow employees. There would be no business or professional requirement, such as reading or taking an educational course. In return, I asked only that the person taking a sabbatical commit to spend at least one more year with us.

Beth used her time away that year to hike the north coast of Maine, visit family and friends in North Carolina and Virginia, and spend time doing nothing at all. Meanwhile, I confess that until she walked back in the front door—our first experiment in this perk—I hadn't realized that I could hold my breath for five weeks. During that time, we didn't speak once. To my delight, the wheels of the firm rolled on as the team deftly covered Beth's client work (realizing others would do the same for them when their sabbatical rolled around).

Just as sweet was Beth's summary statement on her weeks away: "The timing was impeccable, you'll never know," she said, blowing in these days with fresh winds and new energy. She thanked me as if I'd known all along that like a car stuck in stop-and-go city traffic, after five years a person needs to flush the buildup in her mental engine. In truth, little information exists for or against business sabbaticals. Logic alone says that loyalty runs two ways—an employee who gives her best deserves my best in return. Then, too, as Einstein once said, a person doesn't so much need rest as variety.

Since Beth's policy-pioneering trip to northern Maine, seven people in our small company have earned and taken sabbaticals. One spent five weeks exploring Australia, having planned out only one week of his trip prior to boarding his plane for Down Under. Beth also qualified for her second sabbatical, a landmark award that came up when the five-year sabbatical began to help produce ten-year veterans. The ten-year mark awards six weeks of paid leave, a $10,000 bonus, and a weeklong, all-expenses-paid trip for two to any Ritz-Carlton hotel or resort in America.

Now, what you're reading here makes sense only if you're also reading between the lines. The implication is that in business, how you treat your people trumps what you do with your clients, schedules, output, and spreadsheets. Happy people affect everything else. You might also read between the lines, in all caps, that a company's policy has to be more than talk.

To the growing list of increasingly anemic business phrases like "committed to excellence" and "quality counts"—phrases that headline corporate brochures without figuring into company policy—I would add, "People are our best assets." Statistically, only half of working Americans are satisfied with their jobs. Among the satisfied 50 percent, only 14 percent are "very satisfied." Dig a little further and see that 40 percent of all America's workers feel disconnected from their employers; two-thirds come to work with scant motivation to help achieve their employers' business goals or objectives; 25 percent admit to showing up just to collect a paycheck.

My own journey from an essentially autonomous PR consultant to the head of a firm has been a stairway of very human insights. Chief among them is that without good people—trusted, professional, respected, motivated, inspired, rested people—I have no firm. Early on I resolved to attract first-rate employees and keep them as long as possible, a simple concept in which money factors less than some might think. To illustrate, once when a great employee left us to move back to his favorite state, a client urged me to offer him more money to stay. The client's suggestion was a compliment and a strong vote of confidence, but I knew better; personal decisions ultimately have no price.

On that note, though The DeMoss Group pays competitively, some of our employees willingly left higher-paying jobs to join us. And though every person's decision has its own intangibles, I believe a choice of where to work traces to four essential motivators.

The first motivator is mission. Communications professionals wanting to use their skills to advance the work of faith-based organizations and causes will love it here. All honest work glorifies God, that's a given. Some of our employees, for their part, wearied of promoting grocery store grand openings and hotel conference facilities—work done in previous public relations jobs. They wanted their skills to more directly support Christian organizations and causes, and that is what The DeMoss Group is in business to do. In the hierarchy of a company's reason for being, a day with The DeMoss Group is more than a job description with a dollar sign; it's a mission to do Something that Matters.

The second motivator is a good leader. Not necessarily the smartest or brightest—or I'd have more trouble attracting employees—but a leader fixed on mission and committed to the people who help pursue it. In my desire to weigh my company's every move in terms of its effect on all employees, I pay myself less money now than when our firm was half its current size. I've learned firsthand that people have an easier time serving a leader who is wholeheartedly serving them.

Third is corporate culture, and every company has one: that unwritten code of work environment, people chemistry, traditions, and management style—even dress code (casual dress is almost always acceptable here; and, no, our work has not suffered)—and whether it forces the employee to defend his turf or frees him to help the entire group gain new ground.

We deliberately work in a class-A office park with a view from our fifth-floor offices that, on a clear day, stretches twenty miles to historic Stone Mountain. Why not save money in a single-story commercial office complex? The answer is that all of us, collectively, are willing to shave profit-sharing for work space that takes in beauty. We also value the annual fall retreat for all staff and spouses, prayer and Bible study every Monday morning, snacks and drinks in our café and our "quiet room" with massage chairs and noise-cancelling headphones.

The DeMoss Group culture's warp and woof is collaboration and teamwork. We preach and practice open-door management. We jointly commemorate victories and console one another on anything that falls short. When conflicts arise, which is seldom, the underlying assumption is each person's value. The word that echoes back to us over the years is that even those who have left our firm attest to its rare corporate culture.

I said that money is less a motivator than some might imagine, and though it cannot match mission, leadership, and culture, it definitely factors. The fourth motivator is compensation/benefits: salary, health insurance, retirement plans, vacation schedules, and other perks. The majority of our competitive benefits took shape in an employee committee of which neither I nor any vice president was a member. Our employees are satisfied with our menu-style benefits program because they designed it. They also participate in a profit-sharing pool each year, a tangible reward for hard work, good attitude and solid results for our clients.

The *Gallup Management Journal* recently ran a study that placed The DeMoss Group in a small minority (27 percent) of American workplaces whose employees are "engaged," that is, passionately and profoundly connected. My reaction to that news is less pride in our circumstances than a sense of tragedy for the majority of Americans unable to associate eight-plus hours of work a day with personal meaning, much less joy.

In another recent ranking, our employees' responses placed us eighth in the *Atlanta Business Chronicle*'s survey of

Atlanta's A+ Employers (under one hundred employees). The Best Christian Workplaces Institute ranked us first the past two years among products and services companies with fewer than ninety employees, a survey in conjunction with *Christianity Today* magazine and the Christian Management Association. Other firms, even clients, frequently come to us with questions about our sabbatical program and our corporate culture.

If I had to distill it to an epigram, I'd say that in business, a leader does well to think less about being great and brilliant than being good and appreciative. MBAs, management consultants, and conferences all potentially have great lessons for us. But the best business case study, for me, on how to keep good employees, started with my nerve-racking decision to send my best people out the front door for a while. The point is that I had to make it about them and not me because good people aren't just the main thing around here, they are *everything*.

Chapter 10

EVERYONE'S IN PR

Everything you do or say is public relations.
Anonymous

Take this test: Name someone, *anyone*, not actively involved in public relations. Now, whoever you came up with, think again. In this chapter, I submit that no one, anywhere, ever, is exempt from PR duty. Even without speaking, every person, you included, is a mouthpiece, a critic, a supporter, a case in point, an endorsement, an argument, a walking billboard, a testament for or against something. *Everyone* is in PR.

Most people shy from that judgment, and given some general ideas about public relations, it's no wonder. On the most cursory level, PR is a profession: a firm, a company, a corporate department. Dive into slang, and PR gets a little beat up with stickers like *spin, party line, propaganda, fluff, sizzle*—or worse—all in direct contrast, of course, to the truth, to the facts. For their part, public relations practitioners can get slapped with descriptors like *flack*, *hack*, *slippery*, or *slick*.

The professional world of public relations isn't that big. The Council of Public Relations Firms, based in New York City, has a modest roster of one hundred names. The considerably larger Public Relations Society of America has twenty thousand members in about one hundred local chapters. But regardless of the small universe of paid PR professionals, the actual *function* of PR is universal, and here's why.

As a sixteen-year resident of Atlanta, I most often fly Delta Airlines, headquartered here and serving Everywhere. One way or another, Delta dominates this region. The *Atlanta Journal-Constitution*, particularly since Delta entered bankruptcy court, keeps close tabs on the airline and frequently quotes its official spokesman, John Kennedy. Like a White House press secretary or corporate spokesperson, John Kennedy is Delta Airlines' face and voice to the world.

Some world. Last year, more than one hundred million passengers flew Delta from three hundred cities in forty-six states and forty countries. Business travelers, vacationers, families, and anyone else with a ticket and proper ID filled seats on seven thousand Delta flights every day. Yet not one passenger among the millions, I'd wager, ran into John Kennedy the PR guy; which is to say, despite his title and job description, Mr. Kennedy is not the face of Delta.

Nor is Delta CEO Gerald Grimstein the face of Delta. The airline's public image, its representative to the masses, is not the employees in its worldwide PR department. For me and my fellow road warriors, Delta's corporate face is whichever of the fifty-two thousand Delta employees we personally encounter on any given day: Delta PR is the purview not of John Kennedy, but of every person who draws a Delta paycheck. The same is true of your company.

What about Delta's mechanics, accountants, and support staff? Yes, them, too, because each one has a spouse, parent, child, sibling, friend, or neighbor who, from that association, forms an opinion, positively or negatively, of the airline. Multiply by fifty-two thousand and . . . we're all in PR.

I love my job. I love our firm. I love our staff and the work we do. To know me for more than a few minutes is to know that I am not halfway in my affections. If I may indulge in a little more corporate pride, virtually every employee in this firm's history—even former employees—would say it is the best place they have ever worked. When we hire, work with media, or serve our clients, my attitude and all employee word of mouth tallies up to premier PR for The DeMoss Group.

Big deal, you say, your *job* is public relations—you *should* get it right. But what about the considerable PR that I execute simply by paying bills, having my teeth cleaned, playing golf, going for physicals, loving my wife and kids, and being a son? In one fiscal year, my life endorses or rejects a lengthy list of companies, organizations, people, philosophies, and beliefs for which I'll never see a dime.

A few years ago I discovered Bank of America's online banking and began using it to pay my bills. Why in the world, I now wonder, when near-instant payment is a click away, would anyone still lick stamps and labor through paper records? Bank of America benefits, pro bono, from my new-found and vocal joy in electronic bill paying. In fact, I'm responsible for several converts.

In my dentist's office, the patient rotation is so well-oiled that the waiting room is all but dead space. Such good time management in a doctor's office so astonishes me that I have sent my dentist a number of new customers, which also further enlarges *his* PR department.

Golfers love to pass along new ways to improve their games—or to spread the word on which courses *not* to play, which resorts *not* to visit, and which golf outings to outright avoid. Sure enough, another customer ("PR guy")telling me about a great, custom club fitting center prompted me to schedule a half-day appointment there, leaving with a new set of clubs and a thinner wallet. This place may not have landed me on the PGA Tour, but it is one of the best fitting programs in the country. My praise by now has sent at least a half dozen more people through the same program, including my son, whom I can no longer beat.

My in-laws recently told my wife and me about the

comprehensive physicals at Executive Healthcare at Emory University Hospital in Atlanta, which could double as the concierge floor of a fine hotel. After we valet parked, we checked into a comfortable office separate from the rest of the hospital system and, minus waiting or lines, glided through a battery of tests never far from our doctor's full attention. By now you know the refrain: I've since referred other people to the Executive Healthcare program.

Turning from business to home, I'm a PR guy for my family—my wife, April, and our three teenagers. April and I are in love with each other, and anyone who knows us knows that. We like each other's company, and we're crazy about our Georgia, Mookie, and Madison. To know the Atlanta DeMosses is to know that while no family is perfect, families are by far the best thing going. Marriage and family have been suffering bad PR lately, but among the people who know us, both institutions get five-star ratings.

Looking now at my extended family, a biblical proverb says that "a good name is to be more desired than great wealth." When my father left this earth in 1979, the name he left to me became mine to lose, and I don't take that lightly. Poorly or well, my actions and reputation now reflect on my family name. My son's will do the same.

I once read about a large national conference that filled its host city with tens of thousands of people and millions of dollars of coveted revenue. Regrettably for the man who sent the city newspaper the letter that I'm about to quote, and for thousands more who read the letter, the conference was a Christian event. "I have worked in a downtown hotel for fifteen years," he wrote, "and year after year, the people who attend [this conference] are the rudest people who ever come to this city." Did the conference's sponsor have a PR team? Yes, it did. But press conferences and official statements crumble before one bad personal experience. To the people and merchants in the host city, every conference attendee *was* Christianity.

The poet John Donne wrote that no man is an island. The Bible tells us that we do not live unto ourselves. We all know to what a great degree we form judgments from the people around us. In our many inevitable roles each day, if we wish to be wise, we can increasingly be conscious of our offhand potential to damage or bless.

We can think twice, no, *three* times, before being openly critical, or rude, or angry. In going about the work God gives us, we must treat every person well, regardless of station or potential benefit to us. Let us stay keenly aware of the endless ripple of just being ourselves. For good and bad, we're all in PR.

Chapter 11

AND ANOTHER THING . . .

*Do what you do so well that they will want to see
it again and bring their friends.*
Walt Disney

Wisdom is rarely on tap. Most often it comes by the eyedropper or thimbleful, in an aside or a remark just as easily missed. In these months of musing over comments and counsel that have steered my life, some of what came to me filled chapters—small chapters at that. Other insights are of the thimbleful variety. A few of these I have collected under this "and another thing" heading.

Good Customer Service Costs Almost Nothing

Late at night in our room at a Ritz-Carlton, my wife and I lay staring into the dark as a construction crew working on renovations down the hall hammered and drilled through the night. I mentioned it the next morning at checkout, and our desk attendant apologized—something almost any hotel will do. Then with no prompt from a supervisor or higher-up, she gave us another complimentary night at the Ritz—something almost no hotel will do.

The gratis stay was good for that hotel only, and we've never had reason to return, so the gesture in this case actually cost them nothing—though they would gladly have hosted me "on the house" should I have returned. But several years later, if you are reading this now, that clerk's independent action continues to pay dividends for her company. Perhaps that's why Ritz-Carlton is widely considered the gold standard for excellence in the hospitality industry.

At the other end of the service curve, I once walked into a computer retail store near my office on a mission to buy ten laptops of one model. After a few moments of looking, I asked the customer service rep to unlock the antitheft bar to let me feel for myself the computer's size and heft. The salesman said no.

No?

"I'm sorry," he said, "the computers remain locked."

He could stand next to me, I said, while I held the computer.

Holding his ground, he said, "No, the antitheft bar stays down."

"Look, I want to buy ten of these laptops for my employees," I said agreeably. "But I'm not going to spend that kind of money unless I can hold the computer for myself."

Fixing his eyes at a spot somewhere past my head, the young man said he had no key to the restraining bar. He repeated the store policy requiring all computers to be locked in the display.

I asked to see the manager.

"He can't open it either," he said, still unfazed.

I said, "Let me get this straight. I came in here to buy ten laptops, but you won't allow me to even hold a single floor model?"

"That's right," he said, now sounding like floor security at the Guggenheim. Speechless, I turned toward the front door. Then I revolved back. "You know what amazes me?" I said. "You don't seem like you even *want* to sell me ten computers."

In my opinion, the gap between one five-star hotel and one computer superstore was not amenities, prices, or inventory. The gap was stinginess of spirit, a bad attitude, a mind-set. You can say that the hotel pays better than the computer store, but employee mind-set turns on more than a paycheck. In one case, a clerk's human concern turned disaster into an endorsement. In the second case, lack of concern and a fundamental lack of understanding of customer service soured a sure sale into negative word of mouth.

Four Powerful Phrases

I teach my children that words have powers. "Stupid" and "shut up," for instance, close doors. "Please" and "thank you" open them. As my children grow up and move into the world, I'll also teach them a few phrases that, in my experience, can unbolt shut doors, leave open doors ajar, and cut passages where none existed. For example:

"In My Opinion . . ."

My field is public relations and my role is to dispense counsel, but the advice I give often comes down to opinion, and I tell my clients that. I wish we heard those three words more often from our leaders, but I hope you always hear them from me.

Does saying "in my opinion" show weakness? On the contrary, in my opinion, those three words signal strength—for what I'm about to say, I take full responsibility. That shows confidence, and listeners take their cues from the signals we send. In fact, the more certain I am about something, the more likely I am to preface or conclude my words with "in my opinion."

"What Do You Think?"

In the greatest business textbook ever written, one proverb says, "Where there is no counsel, the people fall; but in the multitude of counselors there is safety." The best counsel givers, in other words, are counsel seekers.

As president of a small, twenty-employee PR firm, my judgment and decisions are colored by the counsel of relevant people—employees, friends, industry peers, my wife—and sometimes counselors less obviously relevant. Only arrogance would overlook advice because of a person's job title.

In years of work with more than a hundred organizations, I have often seen leaders make major decrees or decisions without the benefit of much more than a counsel of one. Certainly a leader is free to override advice—ultimately he or she is left with final judgment—but to form that judgment without seeking information, news, and opinions, and without listening to the dissenting side . . . well, the wisdom of one is not as wise as it could be.

"Let Me Ask You a Question"

"The stupidity of people comes from having an answer to everything. The wisdom of the novel comes from having a question for everything." In an interview on his writing, award-winning Czechoslovakian author Milan Kundera parted the curtain on his technique and offered a tip to everyone who wants the full story: he asks questions. The writer continued, "It seems to me that all over the world people nowadays prefer to judge rather than to understand, to answer rather than to ask, so that the voice of the novel can hardly be heard over the noisy foolishness of human certainties."

Someone else put it this way: knowledge has right answers; wisdom has right questions. So let me ask you something: do you employ the power of a question?

Humanly speaking, it is almost impossible to disregard a good question. Just the phrase "Let me ask you . . ." arrests attention. Try it in your next meeting. Used wisely (only you know if you're using it to manipulate), a question is your passage to new information, more time to think, and the regard of the people you're talking to. In our culture, questions show interest; they flatter. As a business leader, I also observe that good questions sharpen my employees' own thinking, and we're all better for it.

"I Don't Know"

When Billy Graham turned seventy, a *Newsweek* interviewer asked him why, given his mighty public influence, he never ran for political office. Mr. Graham told the reporter he wasn't smart enough. Away from headlines, a brilliant attorney acknowledged that he avoided a certain branch of law because he had failed at it miserably. Unfortunately, though, these men are the exceptions.

Great men and women, accomplished artists, gifted leaders, I observe, who are confident about their strengths are equally comfortable admitting their weaknesses. In fact, show me an expert willing to say, "I don't know," and I'll show you a constituency who trusts what he or she *does* know.

I am not advocating a string of shrugs, needless ignorance, or lack of preparation. But I do suggest that, along with the phrases "In my opinion," "What do you think?" and "Let me ask you a question," is the confidence-inspiring habit of refusing to blow smoke. I would even suggest that people who say "I don't know" usually know more than it might appear, while those who don't ever acknowledge it almost certainly know less.

One of the best things leaders can do for their children, spouses, employees, clients, and anyone else is to make it acceptable not to know. In an atmosphere of honest questioning, people are more likely to collaborate—to shoot out suggestions, think out loud, and discover information no single know-it-all could have developed alone.

Small things often make the biggest impact—thinking like a customer, admitting to not knowing everything, asking for help. Just take a look around then join the minority who understand and practice these simple principles.

—————— PART II ——————

WISDOM FOR YOUR
PERSONAL LIFE

Chapter 12

GOD OWNS IT ALL

*Most human beings have an almost infinite
capacity for taking things for granted.*
Aldous Huxley

I will never forget standing on the lawn in my pajamas at
2:00 a.m. that Labor Day weekend, watching with my
family as flames gutted our large English Tudor to a stone
shell. By dawn, everything we possessed was lump or ash.

I was ten years old and almost the first to escape the
inferno, having sleepwalked, they told me later, down the stairs
and outside. A fireman saw me shivering in the early morning
autumn air and wrapped a blanket around me, while a police-
man gently but urgently coaxed my sister to jump from a sec-
ond-floor window into his arms. The scene was quiet and
chaotic, lonely and crowded, all at the same time.

For a week or so we lived with friends. Then we bought

school clothes and rented a house for nine months before moving again. I still shake my head to think that long before home alarms were standard, all nine of us awoke from deep sleep and escaped virtually unharmed.

Plenty of fire stories end differently. One recent Halloween night, my friend Bruce and his wife took their kids through our neighborhood while Bruce's father-in-law stayed behind to pass out candy to trick-or-treaters. Bruce and his family returned to find their home ablaze, too late to save his children's grandfather. The next day when I walked around Bruce's charred lot, the smell of sodden ashes shot me back some thirty years to my own family's tragedy.

Good insurance policies can replace bricks and furniture, and families can rebuild. But no policy can replace the loss of life or special possessions—irreplaceable losses have more to do with family value than market value.

I think now of the final days of 2004, as a two-hundred-foot wave in Southeast Asia sucked away people and lives, first in the tens of thousands, then in the hundreds of thousands. Untold thousands more children and adults were displaced or lost. Only a handful of months later, a level-five hurricane hit a level-three levee and death rose and surged across New Orleans and the American Gulf Coast.

One evening of network news should be enough to convince us that personal ownership is at best temporary. To the degree that we know and accept that, life holds considerably less surprise or stress. To the degree that we cannot accept it, our possessions own us.

⁓

In the early days after Hurricane Katrina, I twice visited the Gulf Coast. On one trip I toured a large basketball arena in Shreveport, Louisiana, that had been converted into a makeshift shelter for hundreds of uprooted families. Alongside Franklin Graham, whose Samaritan's Purse relief organization was quick to bring emergency supplies and transitional housing to the region, we walked up and down rows of cots, talking and listening and praying with people who had lost everything.

Many of the cots had Bibles on them, and many of the Bibles were being openly consulted. Now and again, as we spoke to people, we heard comments like these: "At least we're alive." "God is taking care of us." "The other stuff doesn't matter." The people we'd come to encourage gave us a true bead on where our treasure lies.

About six months later, I had a second unforgettable experience in New Orleans. I was touring St. Bernard Parish and the Lower Ninth Ward, again with Franklin, and now with his father, Billy Graham. Some two hundred churches had invited them to hold an event called Celebration of Hope. Up one deserted street and down another, we crisscrossed neighborhoods hardest hit by the mighty Mississippi and Lake Pontchartrain.

About a block inland from Industrial Canal and a few blocks from where President Bush had just toured a few hours earlier, we climbed out of our vehicle to walk at the intersection of Forstall and Galvez streets. From somewhere nearby came the incessant clanging of steel beams being driven deep into the ground to erect new levees. Before us, a small crowd of media had assembled to ask Mr. Graham for his impressions of what he had just seen.

"Mr. Graham, what can we learn from Katrina?" The eighty-seven-year-old statesman heard the question and without a pause said: "That there's much more to life than material things." Unless that is true, hundreds of thousands of Gulf Coast residents had no reason to wake up and face another day. Triumph over adversity, after all, is the real American Dream.

But leave the Gulf Coast, travel across much of the nation, and that dream is almost impossible to see for all our *stuff*. We build stock portfolios, acquire multiple mortgages, deny ourselves no car or technology, wield plastic at the shopping malls, and pay by the month to store the rest of it off-site. When parents and grandparents die, we contest the wills and jockey for more.

Meanwhile, a deceptively small book called Job tells the story of "the greatest man among all the people of the East," a desert magnate with seven sons and three daughters, seven thousand sheep, three thousand camels, five hundred oxen, five hundred donkeys, and an army of servants. As the Old Testament tells it, Satan singled out Job for affliction, and God permitted Satan to take everything but his life.

In quick succession, bandits, fire, hurricane, and disease took Job's family, herds, land, and health. As the bad news blew in with a series of messengers, Job murmured: "Naked I came from my mother's womb, and naked shall I return there. The LORD gave, and the LORD has taken away; blessed be the name of the LORD." The next verse says: "In all this Job did not sin nor charge God with wrong."

King Solomon writes in Ecclesiastes, "When God gives any man wealth and possessions, and enables him to enjoy them, to accept his lot and be happy in his work—this is a gift of God."

My life today is blessed with wealth: I have a good business, a wonderful wife, three precious children, and excellent health. Amid all that, to try to live conscious of God's full ownership has several effects. First, it makes me thankful to the Creator, who owes me nothing yet gives me everything. What can I have but gratitude?

Second, it gives me purpose. Just as money managers invest and oversee the resources entrusted to their care, I see that God has made me a steward, or fiduciary, with a mandate to invest wisely, spend carefully, and waste none of the resources in my care.

Third, awareness of God's ownership opens my hands, loosening my grip on *stuff.* The standard, "How much should I give?" gives way to "How much should I *keep*?"

Of course we grieved that night to see every earthly possession waft away in flames and smoke. And of course the swiftness and scope of the damage brought challenges. But my father's practice of giving away more than he kept had long affected the rest of us, and ultimately, sharpened our perspective on *things.* The fire more finely reminded us who owns what. After all, that wasn't really *our* house.

Chapter 13

THE WISDOM OF FIRSTS

*I feel it is far better to begin with God,
to see His face first, to get my soul near Him
before it is near another.*
E. M. Bounds

The most successful man I've ever known was my father,
Arthur S. DeMoss. Aside from my own estimation of
him, his innovations in direct-response marketing of individual life and health insurance launched the National Liberty
Corporation and its five companies and subsidiaries. The
little business he started at his kitchen table was, when he
died twenty years later, the largest mass marketer of individual life and health insurance in the world.

To what did my father attribute his success? Enough
people must have asked him that he eventually wrote it
down. Yet for all he did with his life, his answer filled only a
booklet that he entitled *God's Secret of Success*. Since his death,

that deceptively small treatise, just a vest-pocket size, has played large in lives around the world. If I were to give you the contents right now, you might say: "That's *it*?" But if you were to take the points seriously, weave them into your life and practice them personally, I believe you'd eventually be most amazed that they had ever seemed so small.

The First Hour of the Day

My father believed the gate to success swung open in the morning, in the day's uncluttered hour, when he talked to God through prayer and listened to God as he read the Bible. Some people give that tip a double take. The head of a booming corporation didn't head straight to the morning paper? In fact, we didn't take the newspaper. No TV? Surely a little morning news in the background? No TV set, either. At least he checked the stock market? Again, no. As fixed as brushing his teeth or eating breakfast, before business, Dad was with God.

The great nineteenth-century British preacher Charles Spurgeon believed that only a fool would fail to post a guard on the gate of the day. "It should be our rule never to see the face of men before first seeing the face of God," Spurgeon said. "The morning watch anchors the soul so that it will not very readily drift far away from God during the day . . . He who rushes from his bed to his business without first spending time with God is as foolish as though he had not washed or dressed, and as unwise as one dashing to battle without arms or armor."

I was only seventeen when my father died, but to this day, one of my clearest memories of him is that morning routine. Years later, that example would make it more natural for me to form a similar habit, though I readily admit to not spending a full hour each day.

If you're thinking that a person could just as easily get apart with God over the noon hour, you're right, you could—unless something else comes up. You also could do it in the evening before going to bed, assuming you can generate the energy and focus. Or you could hope to steal a few moments here and there during the course of the day. But nothing sets the day like matching our best hour with our deepest and dearest Resource.

The First Day of the Week

Along the same principle, Art DeMoss also believed in and practiced giving back to God the first day of each week. Now that Americans can hardly distinguish Sunday from Saturday (or any workday), to observe the Sabbath seems, well, extreme. And these days it is. If the hours in our lives amount to no more than a series of measurable productivity units, then we'd have to agree with Bill Gates, who puts faith up against a quantifiable return on investment. "Just in terms of allocation of time resources, religion is not very efficient," he said. "There is a lot more I could be doing on a Sunday morning."

One thing about the Ten Commandments has long intrigued me. It has to do with nine brief commands and one long one. Most of the commands are four-to ten-words long: "You shall not kill." "You shall not lie," and so on. By far the longest is the ninety-four-word instruction to keep the Sabbath day holy. Who knows whether God devoted more words to the fourth commandment for emphasis? But who can deny that a day of rest benefits our minds, bodies, work, and personal relationships?

Certainly not Chick-fil-A founder Truett Cathy. If you're a patron of these popular restaurants, you know that come Sunday, you won't be eating chicken at his place. On one of the biggest days of the week for the restaurant business, all fourteen hundred Chick-fil-As are shut tight. If you were to ask Mr. Cathy why, he would tell you that it has to do with loyalty. "Closing our business on the Lord's Day is our way of honoring God and showing loyalty to Him," he has said. "My brother Ben and I closed our first restaurant on the first Sunday after we opened in 1946, and my children have committed to closing our restaurants on Sundays long after I'm gone."

My Sundays are not one long session of prayer and meditation, but neither are they about paying bills, catching up on work, replying to e-mail, or preparation for an important Monday morning client meeting. Sundays would have been a convenient time to work on this book; yet I didn't write or edit one word of it on a Sunday. On this day, I resist traveling, but when I am out of town, regardless of how few hours of sleep I snagged the night before, I want to be in church. At least in my life, Sunday rest directly correlates to weekday productivity.

God Himself offers promises for those who honor "His day:"

> If you watch your step on the Sabbath and don't use my holy day for personal advantage, if you treat the Sabbath as a day of joy, GOD's holy day as a celebration, if you honor it by refusing 'business as usual,' making money, running here and there—then you'll be free to enjoy GOD! Oh, I'll make you ride high and soar above it all. I'll make you feast on the inheritance of your ancestor Jacob. Yes! GOD says so!

The First Dime of Every Dollar

Now for the success secret so personal and, unfortunately, so misapplied that some people might consider it poor taste to bring up—my father also gave God the first part of every dollar. It may surprise you to hear that this concept, known as tithing, was not invented by modern televangelists. Tithing is at least as old as the early Old Testament. Jesus later endorsed it as an act of love, and certainly a gift of our resources is a regular and potent reminder of the Source of all we have.

"Honor the LORD with your wealth, with the firstfruits of all your crops," King Solomon urged. "Then your barns will be filled to overflowing, and your vats will brim over with new wine."

For whatever reason, even most churchgoers overlook (or intentionally avoid) this wise principle of giving. Of the Americans who donate to their churches, only 3 to 5 percent actually give a tenth of their income. A second irony is that we humans tend to give more freely when we have less to hold on to. Among the members of eleven primary Protestant denominations in the U.S. and Canada, people gave smaller percentages of their income in 2000 (2.6 percent on average) than in 1933 during the Great Depression (3.3 percent).

Contrast that to John D. Rockefeller—the Standard Oil founder who died in 1937. In his lifetime, one of the world's richest business barons gave away today's equivalent of $5 billion. He tells his story this way: "I had to begin work as a small boy to support my mother. My first wages amounted to $1.50 per week. The first week after I went to work, I took the $1.50 home to my mother. She held it in her lap and explained to me that she would be happy if I would give a tenth of it to the Lord. I did, and from that week until this day, I have tithed every dollar God has entrusted to me. And I want to say that if I had not tithed the first dollar I made, I would not have tithed the first million dollars I made."

The bottom line is that a giver cannot out-give God. My father's will directed the majority of his assets and holdings into a charitable foundation devoted to telling others the good news of God's love. As his son, I've never doubted that decision.

Art DeMoss's little booklet, *God's Secret of Success*, goes on to endorse putting God first in our habits and first in our homes. The pattern is clear: success is the by-product of first things taking first priority—and you can't know this for yourself until you try it. Try it for a morning, then every morning for a week. Every week for a year, try observing the Sabbath. Give the first of everything you have and everything you are. Then see if you don't have the secret of success.

Chapter 14

A TURTLE ON A FENCEPOST

*We don't accomplish anything in this world alone . . .
and whatever happens is the result of the whole
tapestry of one's life and all the weavings of
individual threads from one to another
that creates something.*
Sandra Day O'Connor

Some years ago, a businessman named Allan Emery drove to Boston's Logan Airport to pick up a pastor from Pittsburgh. By all standards, this pastor was an impressive man, but the person least impressed seemed to be the pastor himself. That impressed Emery, who later said, "He seemed to see himself as a spectator to what God was doing." When Emery tried to credit his passenger with at least some of his church's sizable achievements, the pastor shrugged.

"Allan," he said, "when I was a schoolboy, from time to

time we'd see a turtle on a fencepost; and every time we did, we knew he didn't get there by himself."

Emery wrote a book several years later called *A Turtle on a Fencepost*, and since the first time I heard the title and the story behind it, I've loved it. Maybe because it so deftly undercuts the American pull-yourself-up-by-your-boot-straps myth, which in my estimation is as realistic as a turtle on a fence claiming to be self-perched.

I love sports, and I love stories of athletes who make it to the top with blood, toil, tears, and sweat—still working out after others have showered and gone home, denying themselves short-term luxuries for the ultimate goal. But even the invincible Vince Young, quarterback of the 2006 Rose Bowl champions, was not a one-man team. If you saw the game with the rest of awestruck America, you could not have missed Young's supporting cast of coaches, offensive linemen, defensive team, doctors, and trainers—the rest of the National Champion University of Texas Longhorns.

But what about individual sports? Look no further than golfer Tiger Woods, arguably the most successful individual-sport athlete in history. Golf unites a player and a ball week after week to beat 143 other golfers attempting the same feat. Golf announcers rhapsodize about Tiger's natural talent, his work ethic—he has both in large supply—but Tiger didn't swing to the top alone.

In *How I Play the Game*, he starts by crediting his father (who died as this book was being written). "I, too, started as a blank page. Through my first teacher, my dad, the page began to fill," Tiger writes. "Pop gave me many great lessons, not only about golf, but also about life." He cites his early teachers, Rudy Duran, John Anselmo, Jay Brunza, and Butch Harmon—his longest-tenured and perhaps best-known teacher. And he shares the spotlight with longtime caddy Steve Williams, "who has been at my side through many tough rounds and great moments."

Keep in mind also that every great professional golfer started out as a promising junior golfer. And junior golfers, no matter how much promise, *sure* don't make it alone (which my golfer son knows well). They are driven to tournaments, followed around the course for hours, fed, coached, encouraged and consoled. Their lessons, club dues or greens fees, golf clubs and balls are usually underwritten by devoted parents. Even then, before the battalions of support materialize, Tiger Woods and the rest of the world's outstanding golfers received undeserved, inexplicable gifts of coordination and physical ability.

Ever hear of Jose Azevedo? What about Manuel Beltran, Viatcheslav Ekimov, George Hincapie, Benjamin Noval, Floyd Landis, Pavel Padrnos, and José Luis Rubiera? They're just the eight no-names behind Lance Armstrong's unprecedented sixth *consecutive* Tour de France victory in the summer of 2004. (He since has won a seventh.)

Though it's true that only one athlete can ride the twenty-two hundred miles of mountainous French terrain and reach the final stage of the twenty-one-stage race to don the coveted yellow jersey, the victory really belongs to an entire team. *Sports Illustrated* explains Lance Armstrong's backup support this way:

> In football terms, Armstrong is the ball carrier and his eight postal service teammates are blocking for him. If he crosses the line first, then the whole team wins. During a race last month through the Rhone Alps, Armstrong did the grunt work in helping U.S. Postal Service teammate Tyler Hamilton win; he set the pace, shielded Hamilton from the wind, advised when to attack and when to back off. He was thanking Hamilton for the help he provided at the Tour de France last year and thanking him in advance for the work to come.

To the casual observer, Lance Armstrong landed on his fencepost by personal willpower. Besides his record seven Tour de France wins, we know that he survived a ferocious battle with cancer and cycled back to greater victory. But Lance knows better; so his Tour de France winnings—$400,000 for victory, plus bonuses—go to his eight teammates.

Steve Spurrier is a Heisman Trophy winner, a national championship football coach, and one of the ten winningest active coaches in the NCAA.

He also votes in the *USA TODAY* Coaches' Poll where, for years, he has given a 25th-place vote to Duke University in the preseason poll. Forget that Duke finished 1–10 in 2005 and is a perennial cellar-dweller—they start the season with one point in this poll.

The famous coach, now at South Carolina, explains it this way. "The reason I vote for Duke is because I'm forever thankful for Duke University for hiring me twice when I had no other job. I tell people all the time, whatever I became as a coach, I learned at Duke University."

The logo for my public relations firm, The DeMoss Group, is a lowercase "d" inside an uppercase "G." I tell my staff—my teammates—that "Group" eclipses "DeMoss." No Group, no DeMoss. They frame "my" success just as Lance Armstrong's teammates frame his. I began my career as a solo practitioner, but I know well the difference between solo and team, between a consultant and a firm.

I may be a self-starter, but I am not self-made. I was wonderfully made by God and endowed with certain abilities, characteristics, and strengths. Then came my parents, teachers, coaches, advisers, clients, staff, friends, books, my wonderful wife—and even my kids. Those who recognize the supporting cast around them will be protected from an inflated sense of self-worth, and will be careful to acknowledge and thank those who lifted and held them up.

The Bible records a beautiful prayer by King David of Israel right after he was selected king. God promised David that his name would be made great "like the names of the greatest men of the earth."

David responded to the Lord with these words: "Who am I, O Lord God, and what is my family that you have brought me this far? There is no one like you, O Lord. Do as you promised, so it will be established and that your name will be great forever. Then men will say, 'The Lord Almighty, the God over Israel, is Israel's God!'"

From the fencepost, amen.

Chapter 15

THERE ARE NO DEGREES OF INTEGRITY

Always do right. It will gratify some people and astonish the rest.
Mark Twain

Seven million people logged on to dictionary publisher Merriam-Webster's online site in 2005, all in search of a definition. More of them looked up the word *integrity* than any other word, and here's what they found: "strict adherence to a standard of value or conduct. Personal honesty and independence. Completeness: unity. Soundness."

Why the interest in a word everyone should know? Could it be that in 2005 so many otherwise intelligent and accomplished people seemed to have dropped the word from *their* lexicons? That was the year:

➤ WorldCom President Bernie Ebbers was sentenced to twenty-five years in prison for defrauding his employees and stockholders to the tune of $11 *billion*.

- Kenneth Lay, erstwhile Enron CEO, was charged with seven criminal counts of fraud and conspiracy (and later died while awaiting sentencing); his colleague and second-in-command, Jeffrey Skilling, was indicted on thirty-five counts and sentenced to twenty-four years.
- John Rigas, head of cable giant Adelphia Communications, received fifteen years for charges stemming from fraud and conspiracy.
- Tyco executives Dennis Kozlowski and Mark Swartz, once drawing yearly salaries in the millions, were reduced to earning $1.05 per day in a maximum-security state prison.
- Even household name Martha Stewart spent a time-out in prison and later in house arrest when the court found her guilty of lying about a stock sale.

The absence of integrity in 2005 swept more than the business world.

United States Representative "Duke" Cunningham's bribery scheme to siphon $2.4 million in gifts from several companies included two small defense contractors looking for their own advantage in the capitol. For his work to beat the system he once served, the former navy ace's loot included a million dollars in checks, a down payment on a condominium near Washington, and cash to buy a Rolls-Royce. The distinguished officer is now distinguished by receiving the longest prison sentence ever given to a United States congressman: eight years and four months.

In what may prove to be the mother of political scandals, super-lobbyist Jack Abramoff pleaded guilty to fraud, tax evasion, and conspiracy to bribe public officials. Lawmakers from both parties dived for cover when Abramoff's plea bargain included giving evidence about his dealings with members of Congress.

In the journalism and publishing worlds, *New York Times* reporter Jason Blair shook the foundations of this media giant when dozens of his stories washed out as blatant fabrications. And James Frey, best-selling author of *A Million Little Pieces*, confessed under public pressure to making up much of his page-turning memoir.

Then, in a sad twist of irony, a book that had encouraged my early thinking about writing this book was exposed as largely a work of blatant plagiarism. William Swanson, CEO of Raytheon, a defense contractor with 80,000 employees and $22 billion in annual sales, first published *Swanson's Written Rules of Management* in 2004 and had subsequently given away several hundred thousand copies.

His board of directors docked Swanson's pay one million dollars when it was discovered that sixteen of his thirty-three rules were actually copied verbatim from the late W. J. King's 1944 booklet titled *The Unwritten Laws of Engineering*. (This was not the first integrity lapse in the Raytheon chairman's office; Swanson's predecessor settled with the Securities and Exchange Commission for accounting irregularities.)

———

We often hear someone described as having "a lot of integrity," but to my thinking, that's impossible. If *integrity* means "completeness"—the Latin *integritas* literally means "whole"—then the question of completeness wants a yes or no response, not *How little?* or *How much?* Author-poet-speaker Sid Madwed said, "Would you want to do business with someone 99 percent honest?"

Before we smugly compare ourselves to past years' high-dollar inmates, keep in mind that soul fragmentation is no respecter of persons. The husband who says he was at the office late when actually dining with a female colleague is no longer whole. Nor is the professional padding billable hours to the client to impress the boss. Nor the woman returning for a full refund on a dress she's already worn. Personal disintegration also comes wrapped in a few dollars, white lies, and one-night stands.

Once we compromise ourselves, forgiveness is available, but something important is lost. Wise people, knowing they are fallible, hew to integrity as the compass that guides, the wall that protects, the glue that binds. Indeed, as someone has well said, "He who is enslaved to the compass has the freedom of the seas."

The 2005 National Leadership Index, prepared by the Center for Public Leadership at Harvard University's John F. Kennedy School of Government, reports that more than anything else, Americans want a leader to be upright: 94 percent ranked "honesty and integrity" as "extremely" or "very" important—surpassing even a leader's ability to speak, give orders, cooperate with others . . . or his or her intelligence, open-mindedness, vision, and decision-making.

In another survey, one thousand American investors were asked if they would choose a financial services company for strong ethics or higher returns. Only fifty people preferred higher returns.

If it's all true, why does anyone guard so lightly one of life's most precious commodities? How is it that in a matter of moments, reputations that took a lifetime to build are forever ruined? The questions are rhetorical but they bear asking.

Karl Eller was a pioneer in the outdoor advertising business and built the huge advertising company bearing his name. Now he is CEO and chair of the $1.8 billion giant known as Clear Channel Outdoor. A few years ago, the University of Arizona honored Eller by renaming its business school the Eller College of Management, where every student comes face-to-face, in cut stone, with Karl Eller's business philosophy:

> *Without integrity, motivation is dangerous; without motivation, capacity is impotent; without capacity, understanding is limited; without understanding, knowledge is meaningless; without knowledge, experience is blind.*
>
> *Experience is easy to provide and quickly put to good use by people with the other qualities. Make absolute integrity the compass that guides you in everything you do. And surround yourself only with people of flawless integrity.*

In his book, *Integrity Is All You've Got*, Eller says that in the ups and downs of his career, he has seen one constant: "the pivotal role of integrity in people's lives. Those who have it usually succeed; those who don't have it usually fail."

———

Huntsman Chemical Chairman Jon M. Huntsman has his own story of choosing integrity, even when it hurt. In this case, Mr. Huntsman was negotiating a large business deal:

In 1986, after lengthy negotiations with Emerson Kampen, chairman and CEO of Great Lakes Chemical Company, we agreed he would purchase 40 percent of a division of my company for $54 million. Negotiations had been long and arduous, but a handshake sealed the deal.

I didn't hear from Kampen for several months. Approximately four months after those discussions, Great Lakes lawyers called to say they would like to draft some documents. They had been dragging their feet—business as usual. It took three months for this rather simple purchase agreement to be placed on paper. The time lapse between the handshake and the documents was now six and a half months.

In the interim, the price of raw materials had decreased substantially and our profit margins were reaching all-time highs. Profits had tripled in that half year. Nothing had been signed with Great Lakes and no documents had been exchanged. Kampen called with a remarkable proposal.

"Forty percent of Huntsman Chemical today is worth $250 million, according to my bankers," said Kampen. "You and I shook hands and agreed on a $54 million price over six months ago." Although he did not think he should have to pay the full difference, he thought it only fair he pay at least half and offered to do so.

My answer was no, it would not be fair to use the appreciated value, nor should he have to split the difference.

He and I shook hands and made an agreement at $54 million, I said, and that's exactly the price at which our attorneys would draft the documents.

"But that's not fair to you," Kampen responded.

"You negotiate for your company, Emerson, and let me negotiate for mine," was my response.

Maybe Huntsman could have accepted more money without breaching his integrity, but that's beside the point. For Huntsman, a man's word was his integrity. For me, the next part of his story is most meaningful:

Kampen never forgot that handshake. He took it with him to his grave. At his funeral, he had prearranged for two principal speakers: Governor Evan Bayh (now a United States Senator) of Indiana and me. I never was personally close to Emerson, but he and I both knew that a valuable lesson had been taught. Even though I could have forced Great Lakes to pay an extra $200 million for that 40 percent ownership stake in my company, I never had to wrestle with my conscience or to look over my shoulder. My word was my bond.

Integrity is not what we do when it serves us. It is who we are in the dark and how we treat people when it makes no difference to us. If forced to choose, I would hold to integrity over intellect, wealth, talent, popularity, or any brand of success. Integrity can't be taken from a person; it can only be given away.

This brings me to Cecil "Red" Brenton of Toronto, known to local motorists as the "Christian mechanic." In 1972, a reporter from the *Toronto Star* visited thirteen garages with a car in perfect condition except for a loose sparkplug wire. Plenty of mechanics used the opportunity to squeeze out some cash, but Mr. Brenton fixed the loose wire and charged nothing. When the reporter pressed him on why, he said, "I'm a Christian." After the story ran in the paper, drivers flocked to Mr. Brenton's service station where he worked another dozen years before retiring.

Twenty-one years after the loose sparkplug investigation, when Cecil Brenton died from prostate cancer and Hodgkin's disease, the *Toronto Star* reported his passing not with the usual obituary, but in a separate and full article under the headline, "*Cecil Brenton, 89: 'Christian mechanic' known for integrity.*"

No need to look up the word this time.

Chapter 16

A PROVERB A DAY

Nothing ever becomes real until it is experienced.
Even a proverb is no proverb to you
till your Life has illustrated it.
John Keats, letter to George and Georgiana Keats

Two prostitutes approached the king's bench and presented their cases. The first had given birth to a baby boy, she said. Three days later the other woman, in the same house, also gave birth to a baby boy. During the night, the second woman accidentally rolled over and smothered her own baby. So what did she do? *She got up and switched infants.* The next morning the first prostitute awakened to a dead child and the other woman claiming her live child.

"She's lying!" the second prostitute cried. "Her baby is dead! This one belongs to me!"

A court session *circa* 900 BC predates DNA testing, and the king had a long docket. He asked for a sword. A minion disappeared and returned with a sharp blade. Gesturing, the king said: "Cut the child in two and give half to each mother." At that, the first woman cried out, "Please, sir, give the baby to her—don't kill him!" "No," the second yelled, "neither of us should have him—cut him in two!"

The king issued his verdict: "The first woman is the rightful mother. Give her the baby."

The monarch whose reputation for wisdom was forever sealed that day was Solomon, son of Israel's first king, David, and his wife, Bathsheba. In the early part of his forty-year reign, Solomon collected wise sayings and pored over them. Presumably when the collection reached critical mass, he winnowed them into a book that appears now in the Bible's Old Testament under the literal name of Proverbs. From nearly one thousand years before Christ, Proverbs is one of the earliest examples of wisdom literature, a priceless teaching tool still considered the gold standard of good counsel.

In my estimation, of the Bible's sixty-six books, Proverbs is the most provocative. More than two dozen centuries before Sigmund Freud and psychological profiling, this compilation of thirty-one chapters outstrips human understanding with insights into sex, anger management, slander, wealth, welfare, business ethics, intoxication, pride, and subtle human fissures as relevant as tomorrow's blogs.

Proverb is a Hebrew word meaning "to rule or to govern," and the only thing better than reading Proverbs is reading it routinely. I'm writing now, in fact, to recommend that you undertake the brief discipline of reading one chapter of Proverbs each day. A single year will take you twelve times through a book that is boredom-proof. Even having read every chapter more than 250 times, I discover new insights almost every morning, reminders of timeless truths and principles for almost every aspect of life.

Billy Graham once said he read five psalms every day—"that teaches me how to get along with God," followed by a chapter of Proverbs, which "teaches me how to get along with my fellow man." For most of my father's adult life, I noticed that he did the same thing. He also read sequentially each year through the Old and New Testaments, teaching me another truth—that a mind and character cannot be left to chance.

To arouse your appetite for Proverbs, you might do well to sample it, which I'm pleased to provide; but before that, a warning: do not be deceived by the simplicity of a proverb. Each is a key to character, and character is the key to almost everything else. In the words of Pulitzer prize-winning historian Barbara Tuchman, "Character is destiny."

Proverbs 1:5: "Let the wise listen and add to their learning." Ladies and gentlemen, to acquire information, much less wisdom, one's lips cannot be moving. Moreover, as we listen to learn, *we learn to listen.*

Proverbs 2:11: "Discretion will protect you, and understanding will guard you." Like an invisible shield, good judgment deflects problems before they can search and destroy.

Proverbs 4:25: "Let your eyes look straight ahead, fix your gaze directly before you." Life's highways are lined with wrong exits, harmful billboards, flashing arrows, and sidelined wrecks. Here, a farsighted driving instructor warns us to watch the road.

Proverbs 5:21: "For a man's ways are in full view of the LORD, and he examines all his paths." We can lie to ourselves. We can lie to the IRS, our spouses, coworkers, neighbors and friends, bosses, personal trainers, and the guy who mows the lawn. But God reads us straight through.

Proverbs 6:19: The Lord hates "a man who stirs up dissension among brothers." Ever seen a group or an office where one person plants friction between others? It's a classic study in group fragmentation.

Proverbs 7:25: "Do not let your heart turn to her [a prostitute] ways or stray into her paths." Seduction tugs you one silky step at a time.

Proverbs 11:25: "A generous man will prosper; he who refreshes others will himself be refreshed." God's golden paradox is that what you give away returns to you in greater measure.

Proverbs 12:1: "Whoever loves discipline loves knowledge, but he who hates correction is stupid." Your critics have information that your friends are withholding. If you love the truth and wish to grow, the people who discipline you have the goods.

Proverbs 15:1: "A gentle answer turns away wrath, but a harsh word stirs up anger." The largest percent of arguments are sparked by tone of voice. If your first reaction to someone's comment is anger, wait for your second reaction. Even if you have to fake it, soften your tone and feel the temperature drop back down.

Proverbs 16:18: "Pride goes before destruction, a haughty spirit before a fall." How you handle loss says one thing; how you handle success says more. According to legend, a triumphant general entering Rome paid an attendant to walk alongside and whisper in his ear, "You are but mortal." In modern parlance, when suffering from illusions of grandeur, apply this statement and repeat as often as needed: "There is a God, and it's not me."

Proverbs 20:18: "Make plans by seeking advice; if you wage war, obtain guidance." The clear advice on seeking advice is to do it. Before you lay out a project, consult the veterans.

Proverbs 22:1: "A good name is more desirable than great riches." A well-known man cleaned up from a wretched drug habit and the theft and lies that went with it. Years later when he was falsely accused, the court of public opinion remembered his record and believed the worst. Moral: it is easier to restore a life than to restore a good name.

Proverbs 26:4: "Do not answer a fool according to his folly, or you will be like him yourself." The next time someone provokes you, overreacts, boasts, or is patently outrageous, do this: nothing. Relax into the silence. Self-restraint won't get you on the *Jerry Springer Show*, but it will steer you past senseless conversations.

Proverbs 31:10: "A wife of noble character who can find? She is worth far more than rubies." This image of a rare jewel reminds young men of what is precious in a life-mate and reminds the rest of us of the priceless fortunes found in our wives of noble character.

It is impossible to encapsulate thirty-one chapters short in length but long on wisdom, and I hated having to edit the list you just read. Just know that if you've never indulged in a source of wisdom that hands you time-proven skills, you now have access to the classic textbook.

In closing, a final endorsement. One morning while I was working on this book, my then eighth-grade son came down for breakfast and announced to me that he had just completed his twelfth month of reading a chapter of Proverbs every day.

Three thousand years after his book's first publication, Solomon was right again: "A wise son makes a father glad."

Chapter 17

THE WISDOM OF AGE

Knowledge in youth is wisdom in age.
Proverb

The Ryder Cup is one of the greatest events in all of sports. Every second year, for four days, America's top dozen golfers face off against Europe's twelve best in a contest unique in golf for its team competition, and a particular challenge for the American headliners more accustomed to individual play.

Leading up to the 2006 Ryder Cup in Ireland, American team captain Tom Lehman reached outside his peer group—his sport, even—to consult with a ninety-five-year-old basketball coach named John Wooden. Most people know of Wooden, the "Wizard of Westwood," the man who guided UCLA to an unprecedented ten national championships. Still, why would a forty-seven-year-old golfer call on a basketball coach twice his age, a man who coached his last game thirty years ago?

The answer is that because a wise man knows his limitations. Lehman built his career in an individual sport. Wooden was first and last about the sum of his players. Random photos on Wooden's apartment walls show individual stars and groups of players, but the coach himself appears in no photo without his full team.

Surprised to hear that U.S. Ryder Cup contenders most often practice alone, basketball's elder statesman encouraged Lehman to keep his golfers together. He dismissed talk of the U.S. teams' repeated failure to live up to high expectations. "I never dealt with expectations. Our team never talked about winning," he said. The legendary coach focused instead on practice, and winning followed.

At one point in the conversation, from nearly a century of living and nearly a third of that time playing for high stakes, Wooden looked Lehman in the eye and said, "Your character is who you are, Tom. Your reputation is who people think you are. Only you know your character, so focus on that. You can fool everybody else, but you can't fool yourself."

The legendary story about Coach Wooden is that a certain all-American center arrived for his first day of UCLA basketball practice flouting the team rule against facial hair. Wooden gave orders to shave and the star balked. "You have no right to tell me how to live my life and wear my hair," the young Bill Walton said.

Coach Wooden said, "That's right, Bill, I don't have that right. But if you don't shave, we're gonna miss you."

Now sitting across from Wooden, Lehman had to know: would the coach really have dismissed Bill Walton? That ultimatum, was he serious? "Dead serious," the coach said. "Rules are for everyone or they're no good."

———

Far from slam dunks, repeat national championships, and notoriety, Lamar Lussi is a legend in a kinder, gentler universe, a fixture at the school our three children have attended since kindergarten. He has never coached a team, taught a class, served as headmaster or worked in administration. His influence on generations of children, however, would be tough to exaggerate. When I first encountered Mr. Lussi, he was head of the school's janitorial staff. In recent years, he has served in his official capacity as director of encouragement— the job he really had been doing all along.

What can a seventy-four-year-old man do for kids sometimes one-tenth his age? Answer: big things in small ways. For the fifteen years we have known him, Mr. Lussi has telephoned every student on his or her birthday with congratulations and a personal prayer for the coming year. Most of the time, his is the first call of the day (he called my eldest daughter at 6:45 a.m.), and kids remember that.

Besides local calls, this gift of a man has telephoned across oceans, as far away as Iraq, to encourage former schoolboys and schoolgirls now serving in the armed forces. His rare investment in developing lives ends only at their marriages, when they begin to grow into their own responsibility for future generations.

Anyone with a calendar and a phone list, I suppose, could dial up birthday calls, but no one else could be Mr. Lussi. To a student struggling, he is a sympathetic ear over lunch. If you're in the hospital, he will sit with you and your family. He once drove unannounced to Florida to wait with the parents and siblings of a young man in cancer surgery. Another time, the director of encouragement was the only nonfamily member to visit a young student's grandfather in the hospital.

Thirty years my senior, Lamar Lussi teaches me there is no higher calling than that of a servant, and the lesson is not lost on my children.

Three of my grandparents died before I was born, and my mother's mother passed away when I was young; but I suffered no shortage of exposure to my grandparents' generation. As far back as I can remember, interesting adults seemed to crowd into our home. Dinner hours filled up with missionary stories, business strategies, political philosophy—

all the topics that combust among people of active minds and lives. The DeMoss dining room table was probably my first brush with the greatest generation.

As a high school student attending church, I bypassed the youth group, where I would be surrounded by kids my own age, to sit in on a men's Sunday morning class where a businessman probably four times my age taught through the entire Bible in a year, every year. His insights to this young boy were like sun and rain on a new plant. I couldn't have put it into words then, but instinctively I was gravitating toward people already thirty years down the road.

———

Speaking now from my early forties, I understand—indeed, I envy—Tom Lehman's visit with John Wooden. As I understand from knowing Lamar Lussi, we are better for our time under life's tall, rooted trees. Some of those trees, like Mr. Lussi, are known only to a local circle of friends and family. Others, like Jerry Falwell, may be nationally recognizable.

When my father died at age fifty-three, Jerry was forty-six and already a public figure. He was among the first visitors to our home after my father's death, and he returned a week later to participate in his memorial service. (He would subsequently speak at my brother's memorial service and co-officiate at my wedding ceremony.)

A year later I enrolled at Liberty University, the school Jerry founded in Virginia's Blue Ridge Mountains, and the Falwell home was as good as mine. After graduation, for eight years, I worked closely for and with Jerry; only his wife spent more time with him. Yes, he's controversial, but from thousands of hours observing him in the rear of a plane, in a quiet office or hotel room, in his home. I came to see what he knows: namely, that people matter most.

The Virginia preacher is notorious for being the last person to leave the building after every service, staying to shake hands and speak with anyone and everyone who wants his ear. He does this even when he is preaching in another state, knowing the practice will delay his return home by an hour or two. Throughout nearly five decades of public ministry, Jerry Falwell has conducted virtually every wedding and funeral he's been asked to do, often officiating several ceremonies in a single day. Nurses and doctors at Lynchburg's two hospitals know him well from the rounds he has made several times a week for the past fifty years. Those he has served never forget it.

Jerry also showed me that while people are important, family is more important. From my near-total control of Jerry's calendar and schedule, I learned that nothing took priority over his wife, daughter, and two sons . . . or his wife's brother and his children, or her sisters or parents. Birthdays, even grown-up family birthdays, trumped an invitation for Jerry to go to the White House, appear on *Nightline* or *Larry*

King Live, or be anywhere else. I learned about priorities from someone who had them in order, and those eight years in the company of a man some three decades older than me have made me a better husband and father.

In July 2003, Bill Bright died at age eighty-one. I had known him for so long that I cannot remember ever *not* knowing him. "Uncle" Bill often stayed in our home during his world travels at the helm of the organization he and his wife founded in 1951 on the campus of UCLA.

By the time of his death, Campus Crusade for Christ amounted to twenty-seven thousand full-time staff members serving in 190 countries, most of them raising their own financial support. Campus Crusade's *JESUS* film is the most widely translated film in history, having been shown in more than eight hundred languages to some six *billion* people worldwide. Printing presses have turned out more than two *billion* copies of Dr. Bright's little booklet, *The Four Spiritual Laws*.

Bill Bright taught me to think big. Even as he was dying from pulmonary fibrosis, he was dreaming, thinking, planning, writing. I treasure the three letters he wrote me in his final five weeks on this earth (the last of which his son mailed to me after his death). They speak of several initiatives near launch, and writing projects near completion. Still sounding his life's passion, he encouraged me to help tell more people that God loves them. Bill Bright was a statesman in a world with too few, and his vision, focus, and gentle spirit enriched every part of my life.

In 1980, Sam Rutigliano was NFL Coach of the Year, having led the Cleveland Browns to the AFC Central Division Championship. Four short years later, after a 12-9 loss to the rival Cincinnati Bengals, he was shown the door. Like most coaches, Sam went through valleys and mountains on the field and off, but eighteen years earlier, he passed through his deepest valley. He and his wife, Barbara, and their four-and-a-half-year-old daughter, Nancy, drove away at midnight from Sam's brother's house in Montreal to get back to a summer camp in Maine where they were working.

Early the next morning, Sam woke up somewhere off a road near Berlin, New Hampshire. He had fallen asleep at the wheel and their little Nancy was pinned under the wheel of their toppled Volkswagen—dead. Nothing else in his life would ever rival that pain, certainly not being fired by the Cleveland Browns.

After eleven years with various teams, six more with the Browns, three with ABC Sports and ESPN as an analyst, Rutigliano came to Liberty University to build a Division I football program, which is no easy task. Though our thirty-year age difference could have been a chasm, we became fast friends, and I saw another great man in daily life.

What I saw in Coach Rutigliano can be embodied in two words: excellence and class—right down to his way with the critics who circle football programs like moths circle floodlights. From dealing with drug problems among professional athletes, he knew something about developing character in young people. Having moved some twenty times, being heralded as a savior and scorned for losing, Sam understood adversity. He knew that "winners make plays and losers make excuses."

A person can't spend time with Sam Rutligliano and not be better for it. I knew it then, and I see it still. That's not to say we can't learn from people our own age, but here was a man who had already lost his first child the year I was *born*.

———

Character, servanthood, the value of reading the entire Bible, people are what really matter, thinking big, and overcoming adversity—I've learned much from age, other people's age. From the time little feet can dangle from adult chairs at the dinner table, one of the best things we can do for our children is what my parents did for me: get them in the habit of looking to the people whose very lives lift the general line of vision.

After telling of a few of those figures in my life, maybe the best way to sum it up is this: our culture's broken compass is fixed on youth; when it's good direction you need, look up someone well down the right road.

Chapter 18

SHUT UP AND LISTEN

A man of knowledge uses words with restraint . . .
Even a fool is thought wise if he keeps silent,
and discerning if he holds his tongue.
King Solomon, The Book of Proverbs

In early 2006 our nation was up to its ears in congressional hearings for Judge Samuel A. Alito, appointed by President Bush to replace exiting United States Supreme Court Justice Sandra Day O'Connor. The Senate Judiciary Committee—eight Republicans and seven Democrats— must confirm the president's appointment in a formal inquiry, called, interestingly, a hearing. In the weeks leading up to the inquisition, senators, when pressed for their opinions on the president's choice for the High Court, invariably would reply, "We'll have to wait to hear from the judge when he's before our committee."

At Judge Alito's hearing in January 2006, each of the

fifteen senators was allotted thirty minutes, on the nation's behalf, to draw out the court appointee on any topic or issue. Regrettably for Judge Alito and the public, the fifty television cameras chronicling the proceedings caused amnesia among the committee members, who forgot everything but the opportunity to grandstand.

The *New York Times* actually ran a bar chart on page one to illustrate the lopsided ratio between each senator's rhetoric and Alito's responses. Only two of the fifteen questioners yammered less than the man they were supposed to be interviewing. One senator, Joseph Biden Jr. of Delaware, pontificated to the tune of four thousand words (about the length of three chapters in this book), leaving only a few minutes for the judge he was supposed to interview. The hearings finally wound to a close, and a sad day for democracy became my lead in a chapter on the lost art of listening.

In my life it's safe to say that I have never learned a single thing while I was talking. My willingness to close my mouth and open my ears, on the other hand, has granted me free admission to a great education. "Let the wise listen," King Solomon said, "and add to their learning."

As the head of a public relations firm, people pay me to advise them; they want me to talk. And while I take seriously that words are my stock in trade, I also know that the quality of my inventory rises or falls with what I've taken in before I speak. In the process, I have learned that good listening is an act of the will and an exercise of the intellect. The trick is to let the moment pass when you might, short term, have the floor and hold attention. To dominate a meeting or conversation is not power; informed, good judgment is power.

Some years ago a prominent international figure was invited to meet with the leaders of an organization that eagerly sought his counsel. When the day of the meeting came, this group's top brass gathered at headquarters, electric with anticipation. Sure enough, the visitor's car pulled up to the office building and the organization's president, obviously excited, stepped forward to welcome the great man.

As the president and his guest strode into the building's top-floor conference room, an entire executive department rose to its feet. After brief introductions, the visitor took his seat at one end of the table and the president began to speak. He began to speak, and he did not stop. Like an artist at a command performance, the president held forth about a vision of momentous effect. He was eloquent. He was in his zone. He was nervous and more than a little enchanted with the sound of his own voice. This movement, he declared, called for like-minded groups to form a coalition to span the globe.

At some point, he might have yielded the floor to his guest. He might have sought the renowned man's insights, let his famous guest say *something*. After all, this man had the global connections and influence that the speaker needed. But the president was busy digging his project's grave and burying it under his own words. In a comfortable boardroom surrounded by gifted professionals, he squandered what turned out to be his only audience with the great man. Years of talking had robbed him of the impulse to listen.

Time expired and the meeting ended. The president escorted his guest down in the elevator and waved him off. As his car pulled out of the parking lot, the one man who could have best advanced the project turned to a fellow passenger and said, "Who was that fellow in there doing all the talking?"

Once when a large church found itself in a crisis about to hit the newspaper, the pastor called a telephone conference of key advisers: a couple of attorneys, some staff members, and PR counsel. From my hotel room in another city, with the receiver in one hand and my pen in the other, I joined the conference and listened as voices on the line shot out reactions, opinions, warnings, recommendations. After everyone else had spoken, the pastor said, "Mark, I haven't heard from you. What do you think?"

My silence at this point was more habit than tactic. But habit can work for you. In a crisis, the right first thing is not to react to immediate information but to gather and assess the facts. As it turned out, keeping my opinions on pause bought me time to craft a better case. And I needed a good case because when I finally spoke, it was to gently and resolutely challenge much of the advice the pastor was receiving.

That was a case when my silence on the front end opened a later chance to be heard, and I'm glad to have waited. Solomon must have known of the human urge to get in a first word as well as the last when he wrote, "He who answers before listening—that is his folly and shame."

The advice to shut up and listen contradicts the human desire to be noticed or known, but not every good thing is easy. To never close my mouth, employ silence, genuinely hear another person, absorb new information, to believe that every moment requires my input is shortsighted and ultimately sad.

Otherwise life is like . . . well, it's like standing on a balcony overlooking a breathtaking panorama and using the entire time to stare into a mirror.

Chapter 19

THE BEST DEFENSE . . .
IS A GOOD DEFENSE

There's one thing to be said about inviting trouble:
it generally accepts.
May Maloo

Habitat for Humanity, one of the country's largest humanitarian organizations, shocked a nation of supporters when it fired its founder and president of nearly thirty years. From the *New York Times* to the *Chronicle of Philanthropy*, a sea of media served up the details: Millard Fuller, seventy-year-old charismatic leader, had been accused of inappropriate conduct toward a female staff member.

As it happens, Habitat for Humanity headquarters, as well as Millard Fuller's home, is in Americus, Georgia, about two and a half hours south of Atlanta's Hartsfield-Jackson International Airport. The many times that Mr. Fuller needed to fly out of Atlanta, the drill was for his assistant to flash an inquiry through the office for anyone else driving to the airport that day.

A ride shared was money saved. Moreover, from the passenger seat, Fuller had two extra hours to read and dictate letters. (I have received some of his airport-shuttle missives.) Mr. Fuller said that until he showed up for work he usually had no idea whom he would ride with—and for years the system worked. Then one day, the only other passenger was a female employee who accused Mr. Fuller of inappropriate behavior.

Millard resolutely denied the accusations. After a protracted and costly internal investigation, Habitat's board of directors, including former President Jimmy Carter, officially found "insufficient proof of inappropriate conduct." But the damage to Mr. Fuller's reputation—and to the organization he built to serve people unable to afford their own homes—was done.

Now, Millard Fuller and his wife, Linda, are special friends of mine, and I tell this story for several reasons. One is that, with varying degrees of accuracy, the saga has been the subject of newspaper articles and editorials, letters to editors, Web sites, chat rooms, and petition campaigns. So I'm not bringing the topic out of obscurity. A second reason is that I believe Millard was wrongly accused.

I first met Millard when my firm was working for Habitat, work that ended before this story and Millard's removal. Millard and I had rendezvoused for a major event at the Georgia Dome in Atlanta where Habitat would announce a partnership with another large organization. As I entered the Atlanta Falcons' locker room, someone shouted my name and declared that he'd been waiting to meet me. For the next thirty minutes, I felt like the most important person in the world to Millard Fuller, and he and I became instant friends.

I soon learned, of course, that the Millard effect works on everyone who meets him; he is the classic people person. Top that with his love of God, and you start to understand how the man's professional profile reads like a Horatio Alger story in reverse: millionaire attorney, age thirty, sells everything and commits himself to the poor. It's also characteristic of Millard that his salary from Habitat was $79,000, far below almost any large nonprofit CEO (and a bargain compared with the $210,000 the board is paying his successor). In plainspeak, I love Millard Fuller, support him, endorse him, and would defend him anywhere.

My third reason for mentioning this story is to illustrate the principle that one should even go overboard to protect his reputation, marriage, family, and work. While it may seem outdated or paranoid, and often is inconvenient, I submit that a married person is wise never to ride—or work, travel, dine, etc.—alone with a member of the opposite sex.

Insiders and Habitat for Humanity supporters can debate the reasons for Millard Fuller's controversial departure (the board drew a fire of criticism for his removal), but one thing is certain: until he climbed into a car to ride alone with a woman who was not his wife, he was safe from her slander.

To say that a married man or woman does well to avoid close encounters with members of the opposite sex, therefore, is more practical than puritanical. Most important, it is *wise*. In a car, a restaurant, office, even a hotel elevator, to shun even the appearance of something inappropriate protects not just me; it protects the people I work with and the people I love.

I once read about a political candidate who was accused by a staffer of spending too much time behind closed doors with a female aide. The charge sparked a couple of days of media interest, and while the politician denied wrongdoing, he couldn't deny time spent working alone with his female staff member. Sadly, a good man's reputation was wounded by at least the perception of impropriety.

In the twenty-first century, compromising situations sprout litigation and media coverage like mushrooms. Public figures know that, and they do well to so conduct themselves that a wrongful charge of bad behavior would immediately incite a chorus of defense. If I am ever so accused, I want to have operated in such a way that a chorus of colleagues would rush to center stage to say, "She's lying! He would never work alone with a woman behind closed doors. I've never seen it happen—not once."

My firm was still in its infancy—just an administrative assistant, a client-service executive, and me—when we hired Beth to head our media relations work. Beth was a veteran of television news, where female reporters on assignment frequently ride alone with a cameraman. In my industry, out-of-town client meetings are equally common, but I saw the situation differently, so we needed a plan.

My informal manifesto to our first woman executive ran something like this: "We will never meet alone with the door closed. If at the end of a day we are the last two in the office suite, one of us goes home. No lunches or dinners alone together. No shared rides to the airport, and no sitting together on the flight" (forfeiting valuable premeeting time). "When renting cars out of town," I said, "we'll rent *two*—our client will reimburse us for one and our firm will pay for the other."

To this day, if we meet in my office and someone comes in and inadvertently shuts the door on the way out, Beth reflexively walks over to reopen it. (My staff also knows they can come in without knocking, another layer of self-protection.) That kick-off conversation between Beth and me was later codified into the firm's formal policy, and though not everyone embraces it immediately, no one has ever questioned its wisdom. Several clients, in fact, have asked for copies of our policy.

"The bigger the target, the more people shoot at it." Ever hear that? I continue to be amazed at the public figures who live as if they don't at least know the principle. Several years ago while attending a large religious convention in a major city, I arranged to meet a potential client, a man well known in certain circles, in his hotel suite. I walked off the elevator, turned down the hall to the designated suite number, and knocked on the door, where I was surprised to be greeted by his female executive colleague.

Like many suites I'd seen during the convention, this one was a center of business, set up with light snacks in a sitting area that included a table and chairs, a bathroom, and an adjoining bedroom. The man and woman introduced themselves to me and we dived into our meeting. Later when I left the suite, the door closed behind me. I'm quite certain nothing untoward was happening, but as a public relations professional, I'm equally certain that if someone had suggested questionable behavior, their defense would have been Swiss cheese.

Having seen too many marriages, families, businesses, even churches and charities destroyed by once-preventable passion, I offer this simple observation: it is impossible to be physically involved with someone with whom we are never alone. While there are other ways to stumble (short of extra-marital sex), and we are all capable of stumbling, I am determined at least to make it more difficult for me to do so.

God built and blessed us with natural appetites and longings. In a broken world, He also knows better than we do that we all carry personal wounds. He knows how easily, particularly on low days, anyone can take a shortcut to a good feeling. When He commanded us not to steal, or lie, or commit adultery, He was saying: don't do these things to *yourself*. Because God loves us so thoroughly, I am certain that *don't* can be a most positive word.

My suggestions to avoid even a hint of indiscretion are not necessarily easy. And as I said earlier, they are frequently inconvenient. But especially for people in the public eye, I urge you to take the hard road. For reasons that far transcend a feeling or a circumstance, we are wise to take whatever extra steps help us *not* to stumble—or even appear to.

Chapter 20

ANTICIPATE DEATHBED REGRETS

The bitterest tears shed over graves
are for words left unsaid and deeds left undone.
Harriet Beecher Stowe

Billy Graham has preached in person to more human beings, an estimated two hundred million, than anyone in history. Few public figures of the past century, even Churchill or Roosevelt, hold more respect. In fact, in the annual Gallup poll of "America's Most Admired Men," Billy Graham has appeared in the top ten a record fifty times, including a record forty-two *consecutive* years.

Would it surprise you, then, to know that the man who has held the world's ear and counseled every American president since Dwight D. Eisenhower has regrets? In his autobiography, *Just as I Am*, Mr. Graham confesses that while he took on the whole world, he lost something at home:

This is a difficult subject for me to write about, but over the years, the Billy Graham Evangelistic Association and the Team became my second family without my realizing it. Ruth says those of us who were off traveling missed the best part of our lives—enjoying the children as they grew. She is probably right. I was too busy preaching all over the world.

Only Ruth and the children can tell what those extended times of separation meant to them. For myself, as I look back, I now know that I came through those years much the poorer both psychologically and emotionally. I missed so much by not being home to see the children grow and develop.

For decades, Nelson Mandela was the iconic leader of resistance for South African blacks under the system of race segregation known as apartheid, and behind his sacrifice, an entire people rallied for liberty. But in 1992, not long after he was released from twenty years behind bars on Robben Island, and before a horde of reporters in Johannesburg, Mandela grew surprisingly candid about his most profound loss. "It seems to be the destiny of freedom fighters to have unstable personal lives," he said. "When your life is the struggle, as mine was, there is little room left for family. That has always been my greatest regret, and the most painful aspect of the choice I made."

At the wedding of his daughter Zindzi, Mandela agonized afresh. "We watched our children growing without our guidance. When I did come out of prison, my children said, 'We thought we had a father and one day he'd come back. But to our dismay, our father came back and he left us alone because he has now become the father of the nation.'"

The tormented father wrote in his autobiography, "To be the father of a nation is a great honor, but to be the father of a family is a greater joy. But it was a joy I had far too little of."

———

Those of us off the world stage live no less in the shadow of things undone: prime hours spent on the road or in the office, marriage to the "wrong" person, fitness and health gone to seed, money gone before the spending ended, children gone before we knew them.

Even in high school, I could see that while a person can live only a day at a time, life tallies and one day presents us with the sum of our actions. Clearly my father's early death shaped my thoughts here. With that in mind, I began to notice when someone around me tried to reverse a harmful habit or lifestyle: the open-heart surgery survivor counting cholesterol, the newly-divorced father leaving work early for restricted time with his kids. And it made sense to me, though I was only in high school, that if a young man were aware of adults' most common regrets, he might try to avoid them.

Don't think that I began right away. My father died at the start of my senior year of high school—not a natural point for a kid to begin preventive health measures. And for the next eight or ten years, other than switching from whole milk to skim, I didn't. If something on a dish looked good, I ate it. Except for four years of college football, I coasted on nature's gift to youth. Post-college, I took a few extra pounds in stride. Post-marriage, I made room for a few more. By age twenty-eight, the few-here-few-there increase on the scales was thirty pounds over my college placekicker weight.

The real kicker was my trip to see Dr. Kenneth Cooper at his famous clinic in Dallas, Texas. Dr. Cooper is the father of the modern aerobics movement. He knows a little about heart disease. After my body was measured, scanned, and analyzed, I had sufficient incentive to commit to a life of low-fat foods and regular exercise, routines I have kept, so far, for nearly two decades.

In my thirties, my deliberate attempt to reduce deathbed regrets expanded to include my family. By now I was a young man heading my own company and traveling too much, especially given the ages of my children. So at age thirty-eight, I resolved that by age forty, I would cut my business travel in half. To seal my resolve, I announced the plan to my wife.

This resolution proved a little tougher. My work was taking me around the world to people and events that, in many cases, were history-making. Client assignments had taken me to South Africa, Sudan, England, Scotland, Germany, Peru, Australia, the Netherlands, Bosnia, India, and all across the U.S. But while that schedule impressed many people, my children were not among them. Moreover, if my status with Delta Airlines threatened my status at home, I knew what had to give.

In the coming months, I began to say no to certain clients and new business opportunities. And it got easier. And the business survived. In the interest of full and frank disclosure, while my travel may not have downsized a full 50 percent, it did shrink dramatically—and I considerably increased ordinary, routine, normal-living time with my wife and children.

At this point you may be thinking that few employees can choose to decline travel assignments, and you would be right. But the fact remains that too many entrepreneurs and executives *can* trim their schedules and choose not to. I spoke once to a young Important Man who traveled widely to Important Places but could not remember what grade in school his daughter was enrolled.

Billy Graham confessed, "Every day I was absent from

my family is gone forever. Although much of that travel was necessary, some of it was not."

Something about the American work schedule is not outright anti-family but perilously close to un-family—we work as if our spouses and children are what we do on those few occasions when professional pursuits subside.

Meanwhile, a world-renowned achiever regrets that every day he was absent from his family is gone forever. Ultimately, we are what we do every day. What defines us is not one large intention to be a good person, or parent—it's a hundred thousand ongoing choices of every size that arise when we're tired, satisfied, distracted, full of ourselves, threatened, happy, reactionary, sentimental, hurried, bored . . . .

We're not talking about New Year's resolutions here; we're talking about every person's option, sooner or later, to live deliberately. Every week, it seems, I hear another personal story of a marriage too early or to the "wrong" person, personal bankruptcy, a destructive affair, blinding stress, tobacco-related lung cancer or emphysema, a child lost to alcohol or drug abuse, obesity complications . . . as many variations as there are people with prime years to waste.

The ticking clock intimidates us, even frightens us but while time is unforgiving, God is not. What lies behind us is gone and consequences are inevitable but God is in the business of redemption, and we can still give him the years we have.

Chapter 21

HERE'S TO NOT DRINKING AT ALL

*One of the reasons I don't drink is that I want to
know when I'm having a good time.*
Lady Astor

John had his first beer when he was eight. He wasn't much older when he acquired a taste for his parents' homemade wine, and then moved on to Jack Daniel's, also his father's drink of choice. He first tried the famous Tennessee whiskey when he was fourteen—at his sister's wedding.

When John grew up, he was John Daly, one of the most exciting professional golfers of the last two decades, an artist whose muscular, fluid swing rocketed balls down the fairways and out of sight. His galleries rivaled Tiger Woods's. To electrified crowds, "Long" John Daly was a cult hero to the common man.

But little about John Daly was common. In 1991, at age twenty-five, he won the PGA Championship, one of golf's four "majors." Pundits had said he couldn't do it because the majors reward control over power and distance. But four short years later, he seized his second major at the storied British Open. John Daly was on top of the golf world and he deserved to be there.

Just a few years later, by the PGA's 2000 season, a fan looking for John Daly would have to run down the world golf rankings to No. 507. Off the course, John had sunk three marriages. His fourth wife was indicted in a Mississippi federal court on drug and illegal gambling charges. His gambling losses totaled between $40 and $50 *million* (imagine not knowing the whereabouts of $10 million), according to Daly's 2006 autobiography, *My Life In & Out of the Rough*. Along this destructive path, he'd lost a blue-chip list of corporate sponsors and made at least two extended trips to alcohol rehab clinics.

After one of John's attempts to sober up and bypass the casino tables, *Golf World* magazine asked Daly if he intended now to avoid the kind of situations that litter a man's trail with divorce, debt, and destroyed hotel rooms. "Honestly?" he said. "Probably not. I want to gamble and I want to have a few drinks now and then. Basically, [trying to stay sober] had taken over my life, and I was miserable. It's like I've said before, there's no way I'd never drink again."

Minus the golf notoriety and the gambling debts, one part of John Daly's story repeats itself in homes across the country. And judging from national drinking statistics, a significant percentage of Americans have more in common with John Daly than with me. Which is to say that forgetting for a moment all morality, religion, judgment, or behavior, and focusing solely on *wisdom*, I believe a case exists for not drinking at all.

While I have never tasted alcohol, I am not making a moral case against those who choose to drink. In fact, my wife and I probably have more friends who drink than abstain. Nor am I offering a biblical prescription for abstinence, as many pastors do. (Arguably, except for kings, princes, and priests, the Bible doesn't prohibit the consumption of alcohol; it proscribes intoxication.) Rather than preach that drinking is wrong, those concerned about the effects of alcohol might do better to point out the wisdom of not drinking.

According to the 2003 National Survey on Drug Use & Health, half of all Americans age twelve and older drink some form of alcohol. A few supporting numbers:

- ➤ Twenty percent of eighth graders and forty-three percent of tenth graders have been drunk at least once.
- ➤ In the twelve months before the study, thirty-three million people drove at least once under the influence of alcohol.

➤ Alcohol-related auto accidents kill more teens than anything else; and alcohol factors into teenagers' next three leading causes of death: homicide, suicide, and drowning.

➤ In our nation's general hospital beds, between twenty-five and forty percent of all patients (excluding maternity or intensive care) are there for alcohol-related problems. Alcohol kills more people than all illegal drugs combined.

A few more numbers:

➤ **22**: The percentage of people age twelve and older who binge-drank in the month before the survey.

➤ **15**: Alcohol users before this age are *four* times more to be addicted at some point in their lives, compared with those who start at age twenty-one.

➤ **75,000**: The number of television ads promoting alcohol that the average kid will have seen by age sixteen (brewers spend some three-quarters of a *billion* dollars on television advertising annually).

By now all moderate and responsible drinkers may have arched an eyebrow. "You're building your case on alcohol *abuse*," they might say. "The issue there is lack of self-control."

Fair enough. But given genetic predisposition, a first drink is like gambling with physiology, and that's a chance I choose not to take. Furthermore, since every known case of its abuse began with a first drink, what on earth is the potential upside of alcohol?

I was in a friend's home in one of the most exclusive country club communities in America. After a round of golf, we had returned to his house. As he headed upstairs to change clothes, he invited me to have a look around. I helped myself to a Diet Coke, fully expecting to see a well-stocked bar but finding only soft drinks, bottled water, juice, and milk.

When my buddy came downstairs, we got in his car and headed for a meeting. I said, "Let me ask a question—do you drink?" He smiled and said, "No, and I'll tell you why. I just don't see how I can ask my kids not to do something I do."

I was still kicking around the idea of this book one morning when I asked my three children what kinds of decisions should go in a book about life wisdom. My fourteen-year-old son, Mookie, said, "I can tell you one thing right now—I think it's wise that you've never had anything to drink." Until then, I hadn't planned a chapter on this subject, but the speed of Mookie's reply impressed me. How was it that an eighth grader saw wisdom in not drinking?

One important reason for choosing not to drink at all, I see now, is in my son's life. When he begins to face *his* decisions about alcohol, and he will, in the way that others' choices have become my life's touchstones, maybe my choice can be one of his.

Chapter 22

AND ANOTHER THING . . .

> *Books are the carriers of civilization. Without*
> *books, history is silent, literature dumb, science*
> *crippled, thought and speculation at a standstill.*
> Barbara W. Tuchman

Finally, here are four more simple principles that have had an impact on my life. I can attest that the power of each of these thoughts far exceeds the space I've devoted to their discussion here.

The People You Meet, the Books You Read

The late Charles "Tremendous" Jones was a business star-turned-author-and-speaker who left audiences with roughly five times more energy than they arrived with. He and my father already were friends when I met him, purely by chance, during the summer I sold books door-to-door.

The afternoon of that happy accident, I lingered in his living room far too long for any sales call. But those who knew Charles as one of the world's most accomplished salesmen will smile to know that he bought one of everything I had to sell.

Of this remarkable man's many evergreen phrases, one rooted deeply in me: "You will be the same person in five years as you are today except for the people you meet and the books you read."

Don't speed past that sentence. For a moment, look back at *your* past five years. In one happenstance conversation, Charles Jones contributed to the rest of my life. A similar encounter awaits the readers of Charles Jones's books. But while you're at it, extend that life-altering principle to any good person or any good book. Pat Williams, senior vice president of the NBA's Orlando Magic, tells his audiences that reading five books in one category makes you an expert on that topic. Whether that is certifiably true I don't know; but the point is well taken that to put your nose in five good books is undeniably to be the better for it.

My parents believed in conversation and books to such a degree that they encircled our dinner table with people who had something to say and raised their kids without a television set. My siblings and I are not all heavy readers—personalities play into that—but we all value the stories and text that lie in people's lives. And we know that TV viewing is a judgment call, not a *de facto* home fixture, and that the soul of a house often sits in the books on its shelves.

After Midnight

Once during college, I arranged to spend the night at my sister's town house in order to stay out on a date beyond the school's curfew. Sometime after midnight, I eased through her front door and slipped into her guest room, unaware that she had waited up to hear me safely in. The next morning over late breakfast, she said in passing that what we do after midnight generally accomplishes little good and often causes great harm.

What is it about the wee hours? Besides the obvious effect of sleep loss, *something*—is it the fatigue, the anonymity of the dark?—slackens our grip on good judgment. We pour another drink, place another bet, click onto a harmful Internet site. . . . In case I haven't said it to my sister, she'll know when she reads this that I wasn't too sleepy that next morning to catch her comment. Now, as a father of three teenagers, I can still hear those few words aptly spoken.

"I'm Sorry"

In a preface to one of her books on etiquette, former White House protocol expert Letitia Baldridge describes a glaring blunder she orchestrated at President Kennedy's first White

House function. For a media event, she set up bars in four corners—the first Sunday in history that the White House served alcohol. It was the kind of gaffe that newspapers headline, and they did. President Kennedy was publicly chastised on his first weekend in office.

First thing Monday morning, the President called Ms. Baldridge into the Oval Office and on the carpet. Did the champion of good judgment defend herself? Push back? Attack her critics? Say she'd been made a scapegoat? Plead ignorance? No, she apologized from the heart. As she tells the story, that went a long way to salving wounds. President Kennedy, mollified, said something to the effect of "Thank you. I just wanted to know you were sorry."

In my personal, social, and business orbits, I've seen deep hurts and potential disasters dissolve in the sunlight of those two words. I've also seen the person apologizing add, "if I offended you" and recharge the thunderclouds. An apology is not about the other person's feelings; it's fully about the speaker's action. The best close to "I'm sorry" is "Please forgive me."

Don't Worry

When I finally learned to relinquish personal responsibility for everything beyond my control, the ship of my emotions entered calm waters. After that, delayed flights, rotten weather, traffic jams, sick employees, and all manner of inconveniences, even *crises*, shrank to manageable size, along with my stress level. Let me illustrate what I mean.

Our firm once was owed $140,000 by a client who may not have paid even if he could. I couldn't control my former client, but I could see to it that at least one head remained cool. As it happened, nearly a year after the payment stand-off began, we made a proposal to accept our service fee in client product, which they promptly shipped. By selling that product at a discount to several other organizations, our firm's year-old receivable was nearly recouped.

Back in the early heat of fees and refusal, I could have pounded the table, badmouthed the client, hired an attorney, and labored over demand letters. But by now I was getting a grip on Jesus's words on worry—that if God has numbered the hairs on my head, if He knew when a penny-a-dozen sparrow hit the ground, in all likelihood, my situation had not fallen off His radar.

A colleague here the other day reminded me of the time she vented about a difficult client situation but failed to get me as excitedly anxious as she was. After a while, she looked at me and said, "Aren't you worried?" And I had to admit that, no, I wasn't.

"Not even that they may drop us?" she pressed. "Not really," I said. Then, leaning back in her chair, she said, "Mark, what *does* worry you these days?" And I heard myself say truthfully , "Not much."

Later my colleague observed that my calm factor had set our corporate culture. That makes sense, and I'm grateful for it. Instead of fretting over who may leave us, I try to exert energy at the point of hiring the right people. If a client goes, I care—but I don't worry, and I sure don't lose sleep. As for the countless small reverses in any given week, I can't claim to have reached a state of perpetual bliss, but I'm fully aware that flare-ups have only the fuel we give them.

My father-in-law once wrote a best-seller entitled *All You Can Do Is All You Can Do—But All You Can Do Is Enough*. I love that title. You see, we can't control the rain; we *can* pull out an umbrella. We can't control a harsh word leveled at us; we *can* return with a soft answer.

There's a reason that Francis of Assisi's deeply human plea is called the serenity prayer. There's a reason that people worldwide commit that prayer to memory: "God, give us grace to accept with serenity the things that cannot be changed, courage to change the things which should be changed, and the wisdom to distinguish the one from the other."

Chapter 23

THE WISEST DECISION ANYONE CAN MAKE

What shall it profit a man if he gain the whole
world yet lose his own soul?
The Bible, The Gospel According to Saint
Matthew

My father used to tell the story of a discussion with a law school student about his future plans. The conversation went something like this:

"Son, tell me about your plans after law school."

"I hope to get a job with a good firm and start making some money."

"That sounds fine. And then what?"

"Well, at some point, and hopefully not too late, I want to get married."

"I hope you do, son. And then what?"

"I want to get a nice house and start a family."

"Of course, and then?"

"And then I want to raise my kids in good schools and earn enough money to save for a second home."

"Right . . . right. What then?"

"Then I hope to be making enough money to slow down and take vacations with my wife and children."

"And then?"

"Well, I guess I'd like to see my kids get married and start their own families. I'd like to see them become independent and financially secure."

"Good goals, all. What then?"

"If I've taken care of myself, I can hope to live long enough to raise my grandchildren. I hear that's even better than having children."

"I hear that, too. Then what?"

"Well, I hope I'll be healthy enough to enjoy my later years, maybe travel some with my wife and see the world. I want to make the most of retirement and pass along my money to my children so they can benefit as I have."

"And then?"

The young man paused. "I guess, eventually . . . I'll die."

"Yes, you will. And *then* what?"

The compelling thing about this story is that it chronicles the standard-issue American Dream. Who doesn't identify with some or most of the scenic overlooks on this young man's life path? Maybe you've long since graduated from college, married happily, are well into your career, and just bought a vacation home. Maybe you're already blessed with grandchildren and an investment portfolio Charles Schwab would like to see. But somewhere on the inexorable line of time, every one of us will face the final "and then what?"

What would your answer be?

The most common answers go something like this: "Well, I hope I'll go to heaven . . . I'm workin' on it." Or, "I'm not sure, but I'm trying to make it 'up there.'" Or, "I'm just prayin' the 'Man Upstairs' will let me in." Some people admit they have no idea what comes next; but most say they at least hope to go to heaven when they die.

This book is about wisdom. Wouldn't it be wise to take steps now so that, when you come to the end of the dream, you *know* what comes next? The wisest decision anyone can make, ever, is to seal his or her eternal destiny: time forever with God—who created you, me, the earth, the solar system, and everything beyond. The decision is whether or not to hand over your life to God, through His Son, Jesus Christ. The alternative is to bank everything on doing it yourself.

One thing about the ol' American Dream: the fulfillment-and-peace clause is a guaranteed letdown. Even the most impressive businesses can implode overnight, sinking millions in stock portfolios and trusting investors. Children turn up with minds of their own and can break your heart.

Dream houses can burn to charcoal. Family members suffer cancer and waste to nothing before your eyes. At the ripe age of thirty-two, Dave Chappelle certainly had his dream. The comedian's $50 million deal with the Comedy Central channel was impressive even by entertainment-deal standards. But the ink on the contract was hardly dry when Chappelle went missing-in-action, only to be spotted eight thousand miles away in South Africa. The hilarious host had run away from the *Chappelle Show*'s entire third season because, as he confessed later, "The higher up I go, for some reason, the less happy I am."

The financial figures of your life are probably smaller than Dave's, but the consequences of putting money over soul match his zero for zero. If a person could buy happiness or peace, this young comedian would have been at the front of the line.

Jack Higgins is one of the most successful authors on earth; his thriller novels have sold more than 250 million copies in fifty-five languages. When a magazine interviewer asked him what he knew now that he wished he had known earlier in life, the rich writer replied, "I wish I had known when you get to the top, there is nothing there."

So, how does a person gain peace here, now? Can there be any certainty about God or where we go after death? First, be certain of this: I am not talking about joining a church, getting baptized or confirmed, obeying the Ten

Commandments, or even living a good life. What I'm leading to is a real, personal relationship with the God who made you and loves you unconditionally; that's right, *un*conditionally.

Some 350 years ago, influential French mathematician, physicist, and philosopher Blaise Pascal wrote, "There is a God-shaped vacuum in the heart of every man which cannot be filled by any created thing, but only by God, the Creator." He then proposed the following: "Let us weigh the gain and loss in wagering that God is. Let us consider the two possibilities. If you gain, you gain all; if you lose, you lose nothing. Hesitate not, then, to wager that He is."

Most people unfamiliar with the Bible still know this verse: "For God so loved the world that He gave his only Son, that whoever believes in Him should not perish, but have eternal life." Those words sum it up. The Source of your life in the first place loves you so much that He sent His Son to die for you and your sin (which is simply anything that falls short of God's perfect standard), so that anyone who believes in Him can secure his or her eternal life.

What could be wiser than admitting your life is not a self-made proposition? What could be wiser than making this eternal choice sooner than later? I chose God's offer forty years ago. If you still have breath, you can do so now. This is a personal relationship for the asking.

I cannot begin to imagine life without Christ at the center of it. I cannot imagine surviving the loss of my father when I was only seventeen apart from the God who promises to be "a father to the fatherless." I cannot imagine surviving the sudden death of my kid brother without the One who promises to be "a friend who sticks closer than a brother." I cannot imagine marriage for nineteen years without the One who loves my wife and me, both, unconditionally, as the cornerstone of our home.

I love Him more than anything and want others to know Him as I do. I'm so glad that I can *know* that I am going to heaven when I die—and you can know it too. The Bible makes it clear that we cannot earn our way to heaven, for eternal life is not a reward for anything we have done or tried to do; it is a free gift. As with any gift, we must accept it in order for it to be ours.

Hundreds of millions of people across this globe can affirm the wisdom of this decision. Furthermore, almost every one of them would tell you they wish they had made it sooner. If you haven't made this decision, you can make it today. The act of choosing God is as close as a prayer offered to Him. You can say something like this:

> Dear God, I know I have sinned and cannot save myself. I acknowledge my need of You in my life, for eternity and for right now. Today, Lord Jesus, I repent of my sins and invite You to come into my heart and forgive me.

Thank You for Your wonderful gift of eternal life, for hearing and answering my prayer, and for coming into my heart and life as You promised You would. Amen.

If you prayed that prayer and meant it, you just made the wisest decision you could ever make. Congratulations! As you come to know God, every person you know, Christians included, will let you down; but God will not, nor will He ever leave you.

A good thing to do now is to tell someone about your decision. I'll never forget when our little Madison prayed a similar prayer. Immediately after, she said, "Let's call the cousins and tell them what I did." One of the greatest joys of my life is to see Madison (and Mookie and Georgia) grow and mature physically *and* in their relationships with God— who is as real in their young lives as He is in mine.

Next, I encourage you to read in the Bible every day to grow in your new relationship. Get a translation of the Bible you can easily understand and consider beginning with the New Testament book of John for a clear account of the life of Jesus and His message. God speaks to us through the Bible; and we can speak to Him in prayer every day, any time, wherever we are.

Finally, I encourage you to find other people who follow Christ and spend time with them. Tell them of your decision. Find a place where you can spend time with fellow believers, worship God, and learn and grow in your relationship with Him.

I close with the words of author Max Lucado: "You can afford many wrong choices in life. You can choose the wrong career and survive, the wrong city and survive, the wrong house and survive. But there is one choice that must be made correctly, and that is your eternal destiny."

If today you made that choice—the wisest decision you could ever make—I'd be honored to hear about it. Write to me:

Mark DeMoss
3235 Satellite Blvd.
Suite 555
Duluth, GA 30096

Or e-mail:
Mark@LittleRedBookofWisdom.com

Now unto the King eternal,
immortal, invisible,
the only wise God,
be honor and glory
forever and ever.
Amen.

The Bible,
The First Epistle of Timothy

About the Author

Mark DeMoss is president of The DeMoss Group, a public relations firm he founded in 1991 specifically to serve Christian organizations and causes. More than one hundred nonprofit organizations and corporations have sought counsel and support from his firm in the areas of communications, media relations, marketing, nonprofit management, and crisis management. A number of the largest nonprofit organizations in America are counted among The DeMoss Group's clients. Mark and his wife, April, live in Atlanta, Georgia, with their three teenagers. His father, the late Arthur S. DeMoss, was a successful businessman, having pioneered direct response marketing of life insurance through the National Liberty Corporation, which he founded.